REVIVALISM IN AMERICA

REVIVALISM IN AMERICA
WILLIAM WARREN SWEET

ABINGDON PRESS   New York   Nashville

Revivalism in America
Copyright, 1944, by Charles Scribner's Sons

PRINTED AND BOUND BY THE
PARTHENON PRESS AT NASHVILLE,
TENNESSEE, UNITED STATES OF AMERICA

TO

Shirley Jackson Case

CONTENTS

PREFACE

Revivalism has been a controversial question in America for more than two hundred years and as a consequence it has proven one of the most divisive influences in American Christianity. In the preparation of this study the intention has been neither to defend nor denounce it, but rather to understand it. That it has been a factor of large social and religious significance all students of American society will agree; as to the nature of its influence, however, there is wide disagreement.

American revivalism began as a way of meeting a specific situation in colonial America produced as a consequence of the great migrations of European peoples to the New World. It has persisted for generations because, until recent times, conditions similar to those which produced it have continued to exist, at least in certain sections of the nation. In the peopling of the American continent the transplanting of society from older to newer sections was a long continuing process, lasting from the establishment of the first colonies on the Atlantic seaboard to within a generation of our own time. New frontiers were in constant process of formation, while the older sections were made restless as a result of the allurements of the newer regions, beckoning the adventurous to new and better opportunities. Thus American society throughout most of our history may be characterized as a people in motion. Under such conditions organized religion is bound to languish, resulting in the decline of church membership, and calling for new ways of bringing religion to the attention of individuals, since social pressure is either entirely absent or greatly lessened.

A society in motion is always an individualistic society. It is in a static society that institutions flourish, where the individual is more or less automatically merged into the group. A religion therefore which was to make an appeal to an individualistic society must make its chief concern the problems and needs of the common man; it must emphasize the fact that salvation is to a large degree a personal matter; that it is dependent upon individual decisions. Revivalism flourished because its appeal was to individuals; in a real sense it may be characterized as an Americanization of Christianity, for in it Christianity was shaped to meet America's needs. The Protestant churches in America which have the largest membership today and are the most evenly distributed throughout the nation are those which stressed the personal in religion at a time when American society was dominantly individualistic. The emphasis in the American democracy upon freedom of the individual conscience has given the personal emphasis in religion its great opportunity. And one of the reasons for the gradual decline of revivalism is because the impersonal in religion has been gradually becoming dominant over the personal.

To personalize religion is to emotionalize it. Jonathan Edwards in his *Religious Affections* made religious emotion theologically and intellectually respectable. But Christianity has never been simply emotional fervor; on the other hand it is more than reason and intellect. In certain realms of life emotion is a better guide than reason. And that is true in the higher realms more frequently than in the lower. And yet overemotionalized religion deserves all that can be said in condemnation.

It is an interesting fact that since 1900 Church membership in the United States in proportion to the population has been steadily increasing, while at the same time the revivalistic emphasis in the major evangelical churches has been rapidly declining. This has been due, partially at least, to the stabilization of American society and to the change in the cultural climate. No longer is church membership primarily a matter of individual decision, as it once was, but rather it has become increasingly a matter of social pressure. In many places personal religion has given way to institutionalized religion; inner piety to outward conformity. The emphasis in most of the best preaching of the past generation has been impersonal; stressing social ills rather than personal sin, and the doctrine of conversion, so much stressed by our fathers, is no longer even mentioned in the best pulpits. Numerous revivalistic sects have sprung up, stressing continuous revivals and the necessity of a conversion experience, and they have been in recent years the fastest growing religious bodies in America, especially during the depression years. Perhaps the War, which has already brought sorrow and distress to tens of thousands of human hearts in America, may also tend to revive religion as a personal matter. Whether or not this will happen, of one thing we can be reasonably sure, and that is that the old type of revivalism will never again meet the religious needs of America, as it once did. Also we can be equally sure that the personal emphasis in religion will not be lost as long as we continue to believe that God places infinite value upon each individual.

This study of revivalism in America has grown out of the opportunity to occupy a lectureship in the Florida School of Religion in January 1943. It is not a history of American revivalism; rather it is an attempt at an historical appraisal. A full historical treatment of the whole course of revivalism in America would have been inappropriate for such an occasion, even had it been possible to deal with it historically in such brief space.

There have been many books written on one phase or another of American revivalism, but there is no one adequate treatment of all its many phases. Admirable studies of single revivals have appeared in recent years, most of them, if not all, Doctor's dissertations in History or American Church History. But many phases of American revivalism remain yet to be investigated, and until such studies have been made no satisfactory single treatment of the whole course of revivalism in America is possible.

No phase of the religious development of America has been more misunderstood and as a consequence more maligned than has revivalism. It has been the victim of much cheap debunking and has suffered at the hands of writers who have been interested only in its excesses. In his Introduction to the *Heralds of a Liberal Faith*,

Samuel A. Eliot has compared the development of Christianity to a mountain stream.

"It is," he states, "one and the same stream from its highland source to its expanded power in the sea, and yet it is different in every mile of its flow from what it is in every other mile. It turns sharp corners in unexpected ways. Now it is calm and sluggish, and again it is vexed with rapids. Now it gathers itself into a pool so still that all movement seems to have ceased, and then with a new cascade is recreated. It knows the exhilaration of mingled continuity and new beginning."

Many have considered revivalism as having no legitimate place in the stream of American Christianity. But they would hold, if it must be owned as a part of the stream, that it is at best an aberration or a corrupt branch that has poured foul and brackish waters into the main current. Rather I would consider revivalism as representing the rapids in the stream, and therefore as much a legitimate and essential part of it as any other. Nor have its waters been, as a whole, foul and brackish. Rather revivalism might well be compared to the new cascade which recreates, even though at times its waters may have been difficult to control.

WILLIAM WARREN SWEET

Swift Hall
University of Chicago
December, 1943.

PUBLISHER'S NOTE

The writings of William Warren Sweet have made a lasting contribution to the study of American church history.

The original edition, long out of print, is here reproduced without revision. The bibliography, consisting mainly of primary sources, may be supplemented by numerous denominational histories and other more recent works.

CHAPTER ONE

SETTING THE STAGE

How AND WHY did revivalism arise in America? What were the factors and forces which were principally responsible for revivalism—this new and untried method of propagating Christianity—and what made it the chief pattern of Protestant activity in America from the first third of the eighteenth century to within a generation of our own time? It is the purpose of this first chapter to attempt an answer to these questions.

Religious revivals, of course, are not peculiar to America, nor even to the Christian religion, but are as old as religion itself. There have been many kinds of revivals in the long history of the Christian Church, but the type of revivalism which arose in eighteenth-century America possessed certain peculiar characteristics which have had few if any parallels in Christian history.[1] For more than a hundred years the religious bodies transplanted from the Old World to the New attempted to carry on as had been their custom in their Old World homes. But it was inevitable that a change should come about as problems peculiar to the New World began to arise. For when men leave the beaten paths and plunge out into the unknown the old and accepted ways of doing things must of necessity give way to the new and untried.

---

[1] For a discussion of *Revivalism* as a distinctive feature of American Protestantism, see P. G. Mode, *The Frontier Spirit in American Christianity* (New York, 1923), 45–48.

The first consideration, then, is to note some of these new conditions which faced religion in the New World and which called forth new ways to meet them.

I

The first thing to be considered is the situation which arose as an immediate result of the transplanting of a society across the broad Atlantic to a New World, particularly its effect upon manners and morals.

In the year 1847 Horace Bushnell delivered an address on behalf of the American Home Missionary Society entitled "Barbarism, the First Danger." [2] His principal theme was the disintegrating consequences which inevitably accompany any migration of a society. A society transplanted, he declared, cannot carry its roots with it, for they inhere in the soil from which it sprang.

Transplanted to a new field, the emigrant race lose, of necessity, a considerable portion of that vital force which is the organic and conserving power of society. All the old roots of local love and historic feeling—the joints and bands which minister nourishment—are left behind.

We Americans have been accustomed to overidealize our colonial forefathers and give them, as a whole, virtues which the majority never possessed. We think of them in terms of the best rather than in terms of the average. The vast labor and the rough, uncouth hardships which of ne-

---

[2] Horace Bushnell, *Barbarism, the First Danger: A Discourse for Home Missions* (New York, 1847), 6, 7.

cessity accompany pioneering in every new land will inevitably react upon the people themselves and result in an uncouth and a partially wild society. To quote Bushnell again: As the tastes of the pioneers

. . . grow wild, their resentments will grow violent and their enjoyments coarse. The salutary restraints of society being, to a great extent, removed, they will think it no degradation to do before the woods and wild animals, what, in the presence of a cultivated social state, they would blush to perpetrate. They are likely even to look upon the indulgence of low vices and brutal pleasures, as the necessary garnish of their life of adventure.

Lecky, in his *History of England in the Eighteenth Century*, commenting on the morals of the American colonials at the time of the Revolution, states that:

The most serious evil of the colonies was the number and force of the influences which were impelling large classes to violence and anarchy, brutalizing them by accustoming them to an unrestrained exercise of power, and breaking down among them the salutary respect for authority which lies at the root of all national greatness.[3]

Their contacts with wild Indians and Negroes, the latter fresh from the African jungles, were demoralizing influences upon American colonial character. Living in contact with savages, white men seldom fail to acquire the "worst vices of tyrants, since acts of violence and outrage upon

---

[3] W. E. H. Lecky, *op. cit.*, 7 vols. (New York, 1893) IV, 35–36, 37.

upon them may be committed with practical immunity." [4]
The oft-quoted adage that American frontiersmen considered only a dead Indian a good Indian finds much in the history of the frontier to support it. The atrocious massacre of the Christian Indians in the Moravian town of Schoenbrunn in 1782 by Pennsylvania militiamen, of whom no doubt many were of Scotch-Irish Presbyterian background, is only one of many such happenings which serve to illustrate its truth.

As is now well known, the great majority of the people who colonized the Atlantic seaboard came from the lower stratum of European society, and comparatively few represented the best in education and culture. Fortunately for the future, the principal leadership in colonial America was exercised by the few at the top of the cultural scale and only infrequently by those who represented the lower cultural levels. From the standpoint of their relative importance numerically, however, the great mass of colonials belonged to the latter rather than to the former.

The Marquis de Castellux, who traveled extensively in America from 1780 to 1782, noted the indolence and dissipation common among the middling and lower classes in Virginia. They were much given to gambling and had an intense passion for cock-fighting and horse-racing, and it was not uncommon for great crowds to gather from a distance of from thirty to forty miles to witness these spectacles. Frequently they engaged in brutal fights in which the "gouging" out of each other's eyes was considered al-

---

[4] *Ibid.*, 37.

lowable according to the rules governing such matches.[5] Another traveler observed that "Indians and Negroes they scarcely consider as human species" and acts of violence upon them even to murder were scarcely ever punished. The Slave codes of both South Carolina and Virginia did not provide a penalty for a master killing a slave as a result of punishment.[6] Everett Dick in his *Vanguards of the Frontier* records the observation of a trapper that: "It is easy to make a savage of a civilized man, but impossible to make a civilized man of a savage in one generation."[7]

The penetrating observations of Crèvecoeur in his *Letters*[8] concerning the type of people that have, to a large degree, peopled America may well be quoted here:

The rich stay in Europe, it is only the middling and the poor that emigrate. In this great American Asylum, the poor of Europe have by some means met together, and in consequence, of various causes; to what purpose should they ask one another, of what countrymen they are? Alas, two thirds of

---

[5] Marquis de Castellux, *Travels in North America* . . . 1780, 1781, 1782, etc. (Dublin, 1787) II, 192–193. For a vivid description of a gouging match in Virginia see Thomas Ashe, *Travels in America Performed in 1806* (New York, 1811), Letter 11.

[6] W. W. Hening, *Statutes at Large . . . Laws of Virginia*, etc. . . . 1619–1792. (Richmond, 1819–1823), III, 33; David J. McCord, *Statutes at Large of South Carolina*, 13 vols. (Columbia, 1846–1866), VIII, 345. Quoted in L. J. Greene, *The Negro in Colonial New England, 1620–1776* (New York, 1942), 143.

[7] Everett N. Dick, *op. cit.* (New York, 1941), 512.

[8] Crèvecoeur, *Letters from an American Farmer* (London, 1782), 52–55. Michel Guillaume Jean de Crèvecoeur was a native of France, served under Montcalm in the French and Indian War, and made explorations for New France around the Great Lakes. He came to New York following the War, married an American girl and settled in Orange County, New York, where he became a frontier farmer.

them had no country. Can a wretch who wanders about, who works and starves . . . can that man call England or any other kingdom his country? A country that had no bread for him, whose fields procured him no harvest, who met nothing but the frowns of the rich, the severity of the laws, with jails and punishments; who owned not a single foot of the extensive surface of this planet. No, urged by a variety of motives, here they come . . .

Crèvecoeur's description of conditions among the first settlers in the process of pioneering was based upon his own experience and observation:

We now arrive near the great woods, near the last inhabited districts; there men seem to be placed beyond the reach of government, which in some measure leaves them to themselves . . . as they were driven there by misfortune, necessity of beginnings, desire of acquiring large tracts of land, idleness, frequent want of economy, ancient debts; the reunion of such people does not afford a very pleasing spectacle. . . . The few magistrates they have, are in general little better than the rest; they are often in a perfect state of war; that of man against man, sometimes decided by blows, sometimes by means of law . . . men are wholly left dependent upon their native tempers, and on the spur of uncertain industry, which often fails when not sanctified by the efficacy of a few moral rules. There, remote from the power of example, and check of shame, many families exhibit the most hideous parts of society.[9]

In the ancient story, recorded in the Book of Genesis,

---

[9] *Ibid.*, 58–60.

of the migration of Abraham and his family with their servants, from Ur of the Chaldees into the land of Canaan, a wild and uncivilized region, we are told that it was not long until the rude conditions under which they were compelled to live led to semi-barbarism. Lot, Abraham's nephew, was one of the first victims. Unfortified by any [10] strong attachment to the religion of his fathers and with the restraints of the old Chaldean society removed, he fell into loose habits and in the end, according to the tradition, he and his family became the progenitors of the wild race of the Moabites, the degraded worshippers of Baal Peor. The demoralizing effects of migration may also be traced in the establishment of the colonies of the Greeks, the Carthaginians and the Romans. Similar results are also seen in the story of the Spanish and Portuguese settlement of Central and South America, where for several generations there was a steady decay of society and a general prostration of social and political order.

Perhaps no immigrant society ever resisted more successfully the effects of their immigration than did New England. This was due to the type of leadership which such men as Bradford, Brewster, Winthrop, the Mathers and the Cottons furnished. It has been stated that, "such a consentration of educated men in a new settlement, in proportion to the population, has never occurred before or since." [11] But in spite of this fact, the early New England-

---

[10] See article in James Hastings, *A Dictionary of the Bible*, III, 150–152, on "Lot," by S. R. Driver.

[11] M. W. Jernegan, *The American Colonies, 1492–1750* (New York, 1929), 189.

ers, faced with the coarse and rude conditions of life, soon began to display a decided decline in manners and morals, particularly manifest in the second and third generations. In 1679 the Congregational churches of New England met in a Reforming Synod, called because of what was termed the "decay in religion." Some of the evils listed by the Synod were "imprecation in ordinary discourse," "intemperance," "want of truth and promise breaking," and a long list of other gross evils, indicating that New England society was on the down grade. The extent of intemperance may be visualized when it is recalled that in 1731, in Boston alone, a million and a quarter gallons of rum were manufactured, much of it for home consumption. And busy rum mills were turning out their liquid poison in every seaboard town in New England. The rum output of New England which was not consumed at home was sold to the slave traders who used it in bargaining for slaves on the African coast. The fact that New England ports were active in the slave trade is further evidence that the New England conscience had been blunted by the experience of pioneering. It has been pointed out that Negro slavery found a place in the New World only; every attempt to introduce it into the Old World failed because the Old World had outgrown it. It was a barbarous institution, and could only have been introduced into a society at least partly barbarized. Nor does this apply solely to the Southern colonies; for all the thirteen were slave-holding colonies and there were none more active in bringing in fresh cargoes from Africa than the New Englanders.

Another indication of moral decline is the evidence that has come down to us, largely through the church records, of the widespread sexual looseness prevailing in New England, even among the most respectable families. Thus it is summarized by Bushnell:

... cut away from the more refined pleasures of society, their baser passions had burst away the restraints of delicacy, and the growing coarseness of manners had allowed them finally to seek, in these baser passions, the spring of their enjoyments.[12]

In 1891, Charles Francis Adams wrote an essay on sexual morality and church discipline in colonial New England, based largely on the church records of First Church, Quincy, Massachusetts.[13] Concluding his study, he states that "the improvements made in the nineteenth century as compared with those that preceded it have been real, in essentials as well as in language and manners," that vice in our time has "lost some part of its evil in losing much of its grossness." [14]

---

[12] Bushnell, *op. cit.*, p. 14.
[13] Charles Francis Adams, *Some Phases of Sexual Morality and Church Discipline in Colonial New England* (Reprinted from the Proceedings of the Massachusetts Historical Society, June, 1891 [Cambridge, 1891]). Adams states that he had reason to believe "that there has been practiced an almost systematic suppression of evidence in regard to it [immorality]." He remarks that we are disposed "to look upon the past as a sort of golden era when compared with the present, but there is also a sense of filial piety connected with it. Like Shem and Japhet, approaching it with averted eyes we are disposed to cover up with a garment the nakedness of the progenitors." The investigator, "not satisfied with such treatment, is considered a species of modern Ham, who, having unfortunately seen what he ought to have covered up, is eager, out of mere levity or prurience, to tell his 'brethren without' all about it" (*Ibid.*, p. 4).
[14] *Ibid.*, p. 43.

The practice of "bundling," prevalent throughout Connecticut and western Massachusetts as well as in the Middle Colonies, is an interesting illustration of the influence of poverty and crude living conditions upon the morals and practices of pioneers.[15]

II

We turn now to a consideration of the disastrous effects of migration upon the religion of a people.

The early Hebrews coming in contact, in their new home along the shores of the Mediterranean, with the Canaanites, worshippers of Baal, it was not long until they were observing the festivals of the Baalim and taking part in the sensual nature worship of the older inhabitants.[1] Baal worship gained a strong foothold not only with the common people among the Jews, but was accepted by the rulers themselves. You will recall the dramatic story of the prophet Elijah on Mount Carmel in his attempt to stamp out the worship of Melkart, and to bring home to the people the fact that it was either Jehovah or Melkart; that the worship of the one meant the exclusion of the other.

A recent book, *Frontier Folkways*,[2] calls attention to the fact that the modern student finds much among the Puritan colonists which "directly parallels primitive belief." The French colonists along the St. Lawrence intermingled

---

[15] In the latter pages of his essay Adams treats the practice of "bundling" in New England, *ibid.*, 31–36.

[1] See the article in James Hastings, *A Dictionary of the Bible*, I, 209–211, on "Baal," by A. S. Peake.

[2] James G. Leyburn, *Frontier Folkways* (New Haven, 1935), 29, 56, 99.

with their religious ideas "endless superstitions, many of them borrowed from the Indians." [3] It is a well-known fact that Roman Catholicism made an astonishing number of adaptations of Catholicism to native practices in South and Central America, and these modifications still persist among the so-called "Christian Indians" in Brazil, Peru, and Bolivia, particularly. [4]

History is replete with instances of corruption of religion among migrating people. In those instances where religion was the primary motive in causing migration—as was the case among the Puritans, the Quakers, and the German sectaries—the slump in religion did not come until the second and third generations. But among those people whose motive in migration was primarily economic, the slump was immediate. Since the great majority of the people who migrated to America were motivated to an overwhelming degree by economic considerations, we must expect to find that what little religious interest they may have had in their old homes was largely left behind in their long journey across the Atlantic, then a much wider ocean than it is today. An interesting illustration comes from the account of the formation of the first Dutch church among the colonists of New Amsterdam. The first minister, Jonas Michaelius, did not arrive in the colony until five years after its establishment. He speaks of the people as "free, somewhat rough, and loose," and when he came to form a church he found that numbers had "forgotten to bring their

---

[3] *Ibid.*
[4] Anita Brenner, *Idols Behind Altars* (New York, 1935).

church certificates with them, not thinking that a church would be formed and established here."

To the average minister today this, no doubt, has a familiar sound, for who among them has not experienced the same neglect on the part of church members moving from one community to another, even when the migration is no farther away than an adjoining town? Every city in America contains thousands of people who have migrated from smaller towns and country communities and failed to bring their church letters with them. It has been estimated that, among the Scandinavian people who have come to the United States within the last three-quarters of a century, less than one-fourth have identified themselves with any church, though practically all in their home lands were members of the State Church.[5]

A number of books have been written in recent years, both by Catholics and non-Catholics, on the general subject of the losses suffered by the Roman Catholic Church through immigration to America. Though differing in their conclusions there can be no escape from the fact that there has been an immense loss of membership running well into the millions.[6]

If in our own time such losses to church membership and religious concern have resulted as a consequence of

---

[5] A. R. Wentz, *The Lutheran Church in American History* (Philadelphia, 1923), 222. Professor Wentz states that "It had been estimated that only 7 per cent of the Danes joined any church, not more than 20 per cent of the Swedes, and somewhat less than 30 per cent of the Norwegians."

[6] Gerald Shaughnessy, *Has the Immigrant Kept the Faith?* (New York, 1925); John F. Moore, *Will America Become Catholic?* (New York, 1931); George N. Shuster, *The Catholic Spirit in America* (New York, 1927).

immigration, how much greater in proportion must the losses have been in the seventeenth and eighteenth centuries when leaving the home land meant a much more serious break, and when the conditions in America were so much less favorable to religion?

We are all familiar with the ancient story, recorded in the Book of Exodus (Chapter 32) of how the Children of Israel, in the midst of their wilderness wandering, compelled Aaron to make for them a golden calf before which they offered up their sacrifices and worshipped. Not only is that story a record of a specific happening in the history of the Jewish people, but it typifies what has taken place many times since among other migrating peoples.

Within the last few years there has been more unsettling of populations throughout the world than has ever before taken place in an equal period of time. Not only has there been great displacement of populations in the countries conquered by Nazi might, but the gathering of great armies and the carrying on of war industry has unsettled literally millions in our own land, and many of them are wandering in the wilderness. What effect this will have on manners, morals, and religion, the future only can tell. But if the past holds any lessons for us at all, in this regard, we must expect the erection of many golden calves.

III

It will not be surprising, in the light of what has been stated above, to learn that from the very beginning of American colonization church membership among the colonists constituted only a small proportion of the total population. It takes a long time for a transplanted society to sink its own roots into new soil and "to send up a vitalizing power into the social body," and the things of the mind and the spirit are always the last to take root. Of the one hundred and one colonists who came over in the *Mayflower*, only a mere dozen constituted the membership of the first church; scarcely a fifth of the Massachusetts Bay settlers who founded Boston, and the other settlements about the Bay, were even professing Christians. In all the colonies church membership was an exclusive matter, difficult to secure.

From the start the New England Puritans attempted to build their church on the basis of a converted membership only. This meant that church membership could only be secured by the relation of a satisfactory religious experience before the congregation. Such a requirement could be met normally only by a very few, and as time went on, the number who could meet this test became fewer and fewer. The situation became so serious by 1662 that the famous Half-Way Covenant was adopted, which permitted a half-way church membership, whereby moral people who had not had a religious experience were admitted to a half-way relationship.[1] This permitted them to receive baptism but not to partake of the Lord's Supper. In the long run this plan did more harm to the church than good, since it was

---

[1] For a brief account of the Half-Way Covenant and its consequences see W. W. Sweet, *Religion in Colonial America* (New York, 1942), 105–109. Williston Walker's *Creeds and Platforms of Congregationalism* contains the fullest and most satisfactory account of this period in the history of American Congregationalism (New York, 1905).

soon found that a great majority of people were fully satisfied with this half-way relationship, while the number
which sought full communion continued to decline, even
more rapidly than before.

The fact that the Anglican Church never succeeded in
securing a bishop for the colonies meant that confirmation
was practically unknown in colonial America, since it could
only be obtained by journeying to England. In a Church
like the Episcopalian where the sacrament of the Lord's
Supper is administered only to those who have received
confirmation, the absence of bishops, who alone can con-
firm, is of course a serious handicap. It is true that in 1662
an amendment to the rubric requiring confirmation before
communion was made, permitting those who were ready
and desirous to be confirmed to receive the sacrament, yet
under such conditions it would mean that only the most
earnest would be willing to participate.[2] The absence of
bishops and church courts in America also meant that
there were no means of administering discipline nor any
adequate supervision, either of the churches or the clergy.
Any church that does not have effective means of administering discipline, especially on a crude and rough frontier,
is bound to gain an unsavory reputation. It is true that the
missionaries working under the S.P.G. were to some
degree supervised, but in Virginia and Maryland, where
the great majority of the parishes were self-supporting, the
clergy left much to be desired and the cause of religion was
undoubtedly greatly hampered.

The large influx of immigration during the eighteenth

[2] W. W. Sweet, *Religion in Colonial America*, 271-272, note.

century was a dominating factor in the religious situation of the time. With the opening of the century England had ceased being the principal source of immigration to her American colonies. For England's colonies in America the eighteenth century "was preeminently the century of the foreigner." [3] By 1760 at least one third of the entire colonial population was foreign born. The Germans and the Scotch-Irish furnished the greatest number of immigrants, though several other nationalities were represented. Between 1727 and 1765 seventy thousand Germans landed at colonial ports and took up their residence in America, especially in New York, Pennsylvania and Maryland. The Scotch-Irish were far more numerous, adding from 150,000 to 200,000 to the colonial population by 1776.[4] Freedom from family ties and church connections in the Old World constituted an invitation to indulgences in the New which would have been shunned in their old home surroundings. It is the contention of sociologists that it takes three generations to bridge the gap between the Old World and the New, and that it is the second generation, the children of immigrants, who face the greatest difficulty of adjustment.

Both Germans and Scotch-Irish possessed slender economic resources. The Germans particularly were poverty stricken. Many of them came as redemptioners and on

---

[3] C. P. Nettles, *The Roots of American Civilization* (New York, 1939), 383. In 1912 only one-sixth of the population was foreign born.
[4] Carl Wittke, *We Who Built America* (New York, 1940), 50; Max Farrand, "Immigration in the Light of History," *New Republic*, IX (Dec. 2, 9, 16, 23, 1916).

landing were sold as indentured servants to the Pennsylvania farmers, and were thus scattered widely. They came without legitimate ministers or schoolmasters and were the prey of unscrupulous adventurers who took advantage of their ignorance of conditions in America, and of their poverty, to exploit them. The story of both the German Lutheran and German Reformed Churches in colonial America is replete with instances of drunken and immoral schoolmasters and discredited ministers imposing themselves upon German communities.[5] Under such leadership there was little to attract the German settlers to the church or to religion.

Even more scattered than were the Germans were the Scotch-Irish, who pushed largely into the back country where they lived in isolated communities. They too were poor and largely without religious leaders and, in spite of the fact that their coming accounts for the rapid growth of colonial Presbyterians, it also helps to account for the growing irreligion in the colonies.

The small number of church members in eighteenth-century colonial America was in great contrast to the general situation in the countries in western Europe from which the American colonies had come. There, everywhere were State Churches, and becoming a church member was simply a matter of living to maturity. Church membership had become to a large extent co-extensive with citizenship,

[5] *The Journal of Henry Melchior Muhlenberg* (Philadelphia, 1942), I. The recent publication of the first volume of the *Journal* brings out even more clearly than the Reports to Halle the disgraceful situation among the American Germans in this respect.

though there were, of course, small rebel groups in all countries in which membership was based on a personal religious experience.

These are some of the principal factors which help explain the large proportion of unchurched people that were to be found in Colonial America. Any exact figures are, of course, impossible to obtain, but fairly accurate estimates are possible. That New England was the best churched section of the colonies goes without saying, and here church membership was about one to eight in 1760.[6] In the Middle Colonies where the great new German and Scotch-Irish immigration was coming to a larger extent than anywhere else, the proportion of unchurched was much larger, and was perhaps something like one to fifteen or eighteen. In the Southern Colonies the ratio of the churched to the unchurched was not more than one to twenty; taking the colonies as a whole, the ratio was something like one to twelve.

Church membership is not always an accurate measure of the influence of religion on society, but that it does have

---

[6] Ezra Stiles, *Itineraries and Correspondence* (F. B. Dexter, ed.) (New Haven, 1918), 92–94. Ezra Stiles estimated that in 1760 there were 450,000 Congregationalists in New England. He obtained this figure by simply subtracting the number of members of the dissenting bodies from the total population, considering every New Englander a Congregationalist who was not a dissenter. At this time there were about 600 congregations of Congregationalists in the New England colonies which would mean an average of 750 members to each congregation. Actually there were on an average very probably less than one hundred full members to each congregation, which would mean that the ratio was about one church member to every seven or eight non-church members. He gives the number of dissenters as 62,420, which includes the Anglicans, the Baptists, and Quakers.

considerable significance will be generally recognized. The fact that the great majority of the people living in America in the eighteenth century were outside any church is proof of an overwhelming indifference to religion. The urge on the part of religious leaders to find a way of winning this large and growing unchurched element in the colonial population to the Christian way of life and to church fellowship was, undoubtedly, one of the principal factors in starting the great Colonial Awakenings.

IV

One of the fundamental ideas which came out of the Reformation was that the individual could make his own approach to God; that there was no need of an intermediary priesthood, since each person could be his own priest. We call this the Doctrine of the Universal Priesthood of all Believers, which was held, to a greater or less degree, by all the reformers and became an accepted doctrine of Protestantism.[1] In Colonial America this doctrine had a much larger chance at fulfillment than in the Old World. There it was put widely into practice among the Quakers, the Baptists, the German sectaries, and later among the Methodists especially. The emphasis upon lay

---

[1] Thomas M. Lindsay, *A History of the Reformation* (New York, 1910), 2 vols. I, 240–241. Luther first set forth this revolutionary idea in his *The Liberty of a Christian Man*. In this little book he argues that the Scriptures make no distinction between the laity and the clergy except that certain men are set apart, and called "ministers, servants and stewards who are to serve the rest in the ministry of the Word . . . though it is true that we are all equally priests, yet cannot we, nor ought we if we could, all to minister and teach publicly."

leadership would naturally arise in any region where there was a scarcity of professionally trained and regularly ordained ministers and a lack of feeling for the organized church and established churchly tradition.[2]

One of the great influences upon organized religion coming out of the general colonial environment was the personalizing of religion. In the Old World religion was largely an institutional matter rather than an individual concern. There salvation was achieved through the church rather than through individual effort. In the colonies, on the other hand, the exact opposite was true. In none of them, even in those in which there were State Churches, did salvation become institutionalized although, after the adoption of the Half-Way Covenant in New England, the tendency was in that direction.

Preaching, likewise, among all the colonial religious bodies came largely to deal with individual needs. In the stress and strain of colonization, where the facing of hardships was an every-day experience, there was a demand for a type of religion and preaching that would concern itself with everyday needs and individual concerns. Calvinism is a legalistic system and the tendency of the early Calvinistic clergy was to devote their sermons to an exposition and defense of the system, but in the course of time the legalistic theology of Calvinism became in the hands of men like Edwards and Tennent a personalized Calvinism searching out the hearts of individuals. The individualistic emphasis

---

[2] For the rise of the lay influence in Colonial America see T. C. Hall, *The Religious Background of American Culture* (Boston, 1930), 155–156; other references under "Lay element."

in colonial religion will be the principal theme of the next chapter.

v

A last factor which helped set the stage for colonial revivalism was the growing awareness and concern on the part of colonial religious leaders of the decline of religion and morality among the colonists. No great improvement in religion ever came about by chance.

That the colonial religious leaders were painfully aware of the sad state of religion in the latter seventeenth and early eighteenth centuries we have abundant testimony. The election sermons preached every year in each of the New England colonies are filled with gloomy forebodings because of the low state of religion and public morals. Some of the sermon subjects will show something of this concern. Samuel Willard in 1700 preached on the "Perils of the Time Displayed"; in 1711 Stephen Buckingham took as his subject "The Unreasonableness and Danger of a People's Renouncing Their Subjection to God"; in 1730 William Russell preached on "The Decay of Love to God in Churches, Offensive and Dangerous." The vast movement of immigrant people into the middle colonies, especially at this period, completely swamped the feeble religious organizations, as was indicated by the appeals for help coming from the Presbyterian, Lutheran, and Reformed leaders. Times were ripe indeed for a new emphasis and a new method in religion, as well as for a new type of religious leadership, to meet the peculiar needs presented by the American colonial religious situation.

CHAPTER TWO

COLONIAL REVIVALISM AND THE GROWTH OF DEMOCRACY

A MISCONCEPTION entertained by many good people is that full-fledged democracy sprang immediately out of the Reformation. Another misconception widely held is that the largest contribution to democracy in early America was made by the New England Puritans. G. P. Gooch in his *English Democratic Ideas of the Seventeenth Century* [1] makes the oft-quoted statement that "modern democracy was the child of the Reformation, not of the Reformers." Gooch has also pointed out that the two great principles upon which the Reformation was based were "the rightful duty of free inquiry and the Priesthood of all believers." "The first," he states, "led to liberty; the second to equality," [2] but both were a long time in coming to full fruition. A similar statement might be made regarding New England Puritanism; American democracy owes much to Puritanism, but not to the Puritan leaders. In adopting the Congregational form of church polity the New England Puritans planted the seed of pure democracy in American soil. The plant which sprang from it was of slow development, but because there was no soil in the world so well adapted to its final and full unfolding as in America, it grew eventually into a mighty tree.

---

[1] Second edition, with notes by H. J. Laski (Cambridge, 1927), 7.
[2] *Ibid.*, 8.

For a hundred years and more after the establishment of the first permanent colonies in America, religion, as we have already seen, was a matter of the few. The great mass of the people had little concern and less part in it. The principal colonial churches in their organization were aristocracies. The Anglican Church in Virginia was under the management and control of the planter aristocracy. The lay Vestries, made up of the great tobacco gentry, were self-perpetuating bodies and managed the affairs of the parish, largely for the benefit of their own class. A religion which would be a vital concern of every-day life was foreign to their desires. In New England the membership of the churches was made up of a small minority and, to a large degree, was under the control of the minister and the lay officials. Calvin had a very low opinion of the common people, and his spiritual children among the Presbyterians, the Congregationalists, and the Reformed bodies were in full agreement with him in this as in other matters. The Quakers, especially after the adoption of birthright membership, came to be more and more an upper-class, prosperous group. As is well known, the early New England fathers had a poor opinion of democracy and considered it the "meanest" of all forms of government. They conceived it to be their principal task to see to it that the "elect," the chosen of God, controlled in both Church and State. They would have been in full agreement with Gilbert K. Chesterton's assertion that "the majority are always wrong." They considered democracy a dangerous thing in a government such as theirs, pledged to carry out

God's will; for, they asked, "How could ungodly rulers know the will and purpose of God?" Therefore, it seemed to them necessary to keep the godly minority in control and the whole machinery of government both in Church and State was directed to that end.

Such was the religious situation in the American colonies at the end of the first third of the nineteenth century. Religion had played a prominent rôle in the establishment of most of the colonies, but its influence had steadily declined with each succeeding generation. The dominant religious groups were the offshoots of the principal European Churches, and the methods followed in the colonies up to that time had largely followed the Old World patterns. Until the opening of the eighteenth century there was little in the American religious scene which could be called distinctly American. The fact that religious influence was definitely on the wane is proof that the Old World patterns had not met the New World problems.

I

The story of colonial revivalism is the story of the beginning of the Americanization of organized Christianity; of the gradual adoption of new and untried ways of meeting peculiar American needs.[1]

What we have come to call *pietism* lies at the heart of the great colonial awakenings. By *pietism* we mean a type of religion which places the principal emphasis upon what

---

[1] P. G. Mode, *The Frontier Spirit in American Christianity* (New York, 1923), 45–50.

is often termed the religion of the heart, rather than a religion of the head. It is a religion which appeals primarily to the emotions. Its principal theme is redemption for individuals. Its object is to awaken men and women to a personal repentance.

The pietistic emphasis was introduced into the American colonies largely through the German immigration which began its flow in the latter seventeenth century and became a mighty tide with the opening of the eighteenth. It came largely from southern Germany, the region in which German pietism had won its principal early following. It manifested itself most strongly in the left-wing religious bodies, which came out of the Reformation and was found most highly developed among the Mennonites, the Moravians, the Dunkers, and other left-wing groups. It, however, gained great impetus among the Lutheran and Reformed Churches of Germany and Scandinavia. The English Baptists, Quakers, and in the eighteenth century the Methodists, were imbued with pietism, stressing inner religion and the emotional response, repudiating salvation through an institution and emphasizing the individual's responsibility.

In the Old World this emotional and individualistic type of religion, as has been noted, found its principal following among the "sects." [2] In all the Old World countries where there were everywhere State Churches, the "sects"

---

[2] For a discussion of the sects and revivalism see J. M. Mecklin, *The Story of American Dissent* (New York, 1934), chapter ix, "Dissent Becomes Revivalistic."

found small chance to develop. There they were generally despised by the "Churches" and oppressed by the state authorities. In Colonial America, on the other hand, they found opportunity for growth and expansion, and the individualistic emphasis in pioneering gave them an opportunity such as could not have been found anywhere else in all the world.

II

It has been frequently stated that the great colonial revival, which swept over the colonies from New England to Georgia in the middle third of the eighteenth century, was the extension of the great evangelical revival in England, fathered by the Wesleys and Whitefield. That this is an erroneous statement is easily shown by the mere fact that the pietistic revival among the Dutch Reformed people in New Jersey was at high tide (1726) twelve years before John Wesley had his heart-warming experience at Aldersgate, and, in that very year (1738) the revivalistic Presbyterians formed the New Brunswick Presbytery in order to give greater impetus to the revivals which were mounting higher and higher throughout that whole region.

Theodore J. Frelinghuysen,[1] the leader of the revivalistic movement among the Dutch Reformed people, was a pietist, thoroughly imbued with pietistic principles before coming to the New World. From the very beginning of his ministry in the Raritan Valley, he stressed experimental

---

[1] Peter H. B. Frelinghuysen, Jr., *Theodorus Jacobus Frelinghuysen* (Princeton, 1838), chapters ii and iii especially.

rather than formal religion and advocated an emotional and individualistic approach rather than the intellectual. His manner of preaching was impassioned. The communities in central New Jersey, where the three congregations to which he ministered were located, were rough and boorish, and religiously the people had little desire beyond an outward conformity to the accepted religious rites. The Church to them was little more than a symbol of their Dutch nationality. To have a religion that would stir their emotions and set up high standards of personal conduct was the last thing that most of them desired. The well-to-do, the kind who generally gain control of institutionalized religion, were bitterly opposed to Frelinghuysen and all his ways; the poorer class and the younger generation were attracted to the young and vivid dominie. The result was a bitter clash which soon had reverberations in every Dutch congregation in America and even reached Holland.[2] Eventually, however, the revivalistic or pietistic element in the Dutch Church gained a majority, though the controversy continued until the very end of the colonial period.

What took place among the Dutch Churches in Colonial America was typical of the effect of revivalism among all the institutionalized religious bodies in which it gained a foothold. Though causing long and bitter controversy, the individualized emphasis in the Dutch Church saved it from complete extinction in Colonial America.

---

[2] See also chapter iii, "Theodore J. Frelinghuysen and the Log College Evangelists."

The Dutch revival paved the way for the much more widespread Presbyterian awakening in New Jersey and the adjoining colonies of Pennsylvania, New York, and Delaware, and this awakening eventually spread into every region in which Scotch-Irish settlers were to be found.

In the history of revivalism the outstanding individual revivalists have been Calvinists: exactly contrary to what might have been expected. Calvinism is a legalistic system, and logically is almost if not quite water-tight. Bishop McConnell has called attention to the fact that, "There is something impersonal about logic, and sooner or later the logician is almost certain to get the impersonal above the personal." [3] He becomes more concerned about the "system" than about individuals. And for this reason the logician makes a poor evangelist because few people are capable of being reached by logic: all are capable of being reached through the emotions. Fortunately, the great Calvinist preachers have not been consistent Calvinists; and they have gone ahead in spite of their doctrine of election, as though there was hope for every man. The famous Dr. Johnson once remarked to Boswell, that "All theory is against the freedom of the will: experience for it." In their books the Calvinists, with great learning, upheld the doctrines of election and predestination; in their sermons and in their dealings with people they have proceeded on the assumption that every man had his own

---

[3] F. J. McConnell, *Evangelicals, Revolutionists, and Idealists* (New York, 1942), 89.

destiny in his own hands. What the colonial Calvinistic revivalists did was to personalize Calvinism; to make it apply to individuals.

The Scotch-Irish revival was carried on under the leadership of a group of as unusual and interesting a body of ministers as can be found in the eighteenth century. Most of them were either the sons of William Tennent or graduates of his "Log College." The elder Tennent, a priest in the Established (Episcopal) Church of Ireland, came to the colonies in 1716 with his wife and four sons. Immediately he identified himself with the Presbyterians and from 1726 and 1746 conducted a private school at Neshaminy, Pennsylvania, called in derision the "Log College." One of the reasons given by the elder Tennent for leaving the Episcopal Church and joining the Presbyterian was that the Episcopal churches were "conniving at the practice of Arminian doctrines inconsistent with the eternal purpose of God, and an encouragement of vice." This would indicate, of course, that he considered himself a Calvinist. But like Frelinghuysen he was a personalized Calvinist, primarily interested in training young men to enter the Presbyterian ministry and to bring men and women to repentance. That he was conspicuously successful, the story of colonial Presbyterianism offers abundant proof. For, from a small group of struggling congregations scattered here and there in the Middle Colonies and in the back country, at the opening of the eighteenth century, colonial Presbyterianism had become the second largest religious body in America at the beginning of the struggle for Inde-

pendence. The Log College at Neshaminy had been re-
placed by the College of New Jersey, and a whole galaxy
of academies had come into life, many of which were later
to develop into colleges.

New England became revivalistic likewise, as the result
of personalizing Calvinism; when the New England clergy
began to center their interest in a scheme of redemption
for individuals, revivalism was born. And when religion is
individualized it immediately becomes emotionalized. In
the book which is the most self-revealing of all his books,
and his first great theological treatise, *Religious Affections*,
Jonathan Edwards sets forth the overwhelming importance
of the emotions in religion. "The heart of true religion,"
he stated, "is holy affection." He contended that, "Our people do not so much need to have their heads stored, as to
have their hearts touched." And that he carried out this
idea in his preaching is shown by what happened at Northampton. Under it the people sitting in the pews felt themselves singled out. In some of his sermons, to use Miss
Winslow's words, he called the roll of the town's sins, just
as though he were walking up and down the village street,
pointing his accusing finger "at one house after another,
unearthing secret sins and holding them up for all to see."
He made the consequences of God's will seem personal
and immediate; he made hell "real enough to be found in
the atlas." [4]

Jonathan Edwards set the pattern of New England re-

_____

[4] Ola Elizabeth Winslow, *Jonathan Edwards*, 1703–1758 (New York,
1940), 162, 191.

vivalism and a host of others, especially throughout Connecticut and central western Massachusetts, followed his example. One of the results was to overemotionalize New England religion in many quarters, though this must not be placed entirely at Jonathan Edwards' door. Some, like James Davenport, were guilty of emotional excesses which produced unfortunate consequences. Miss Winslow characterizes the New England revival as a "spiritual hurricane." Hurricanes, when they pass over a forest, fell the trees with shallow roots. The tendency naturally is to overemphasize the fallen trees and the destructive effects, rather than the trees that stood the blast and as a result have sunk their roots even deeper into the soil.

There have been many attempts to appraise the influence of the New England revival. The number added to the churches has been estimated at from thirty to forty thousand. Between 1740 and 1760, one hundred and fifty new Congregational churches in New England were formed besides the creation of numerous Baptist and Separatist congregations. Besides this, as Trumbull the historian of Connecticut who personally knew some of the converts, points out, there was undoubtedly a great increase in piety among the church members, some of whom had formerly been "dead weights" to the churches. It decidedly increased the number of candidates for the ministry and raised ministerial standards of duty and effort. Though not overlooking the things deserving condemnation, it was Trumbull's judgment, based on a careful gathering of the facts, that "it was the most glorious and extensive revival of religion and reformation of manners which the country had ever experienced." [5]

Any account of the colonial revivals is incomplete unless it includes George Whitefield, undoubtedly the greatest revivalist of them all. Whitefield, in his early ministry, became an avowed Calvinist which put a great strain on the friendship between Wesley and himself. But Whitefield was no logician and was far more interested in persons than in the legalistic formulas of the Calvinistic system. In fact, the doctrine of predestination and election never bothered him in his eloquent efforts at soul-saving.

From 1738 to 1770 he made seven journeys to America, or thirteen voyages across the Atlantic, and his preaching tours ranged from Georgia on the south to New Hampshire and Maine on the north. In a letter written to John Wesley in 1769, as he started on his last voyage to America, occurs this sentence:

Mutual Christian love will not permit you to forget a willing pilgrim, going now across the Atlantic for the thirteenth time.

He knew America at first hand as few others knew the great sprawling new continent, and he probably preached to more people than any other single preacher of the English-speaking world during the eighteenth century.

Whitefield's work in America was in the interest of no single religious body.[6] He did not have a denominational

---

[5] Benjamin Trumbull, *A Complete History of Connecticut, Civil and Ecclesiastical*, 2 vols. (New Haven, 1818), II, 201 ff.

[6] See C. H. Maxson, *The Great Awakening in the Middle Colonies* (Chicago, 1920), 40–53.

hair in his head and could and did co-operate with all churches and ministers whose desire was to save souls. More than any other, Whitefield tied the colonial revivals together; for he had a part in all of them. He visited Jonathan Edwards in Northampton and preached in his church, and altogether made five New England tours. On his first entry into New England he preached at both Harvard and Yale Colleges. He visited William Tennent at Neshaminy, Pennsylvania, and co-operated with Gilbert Tennent and the other Log College revivalists in New Jersey and New York; he preached in Presbyterian and Anglican churches, in Baptist and Quaker meetinghouses, or wherever opportunity offered.

Whitefield seldom finished a sermon without taking up a collection for some worthy cause; and these causes were as wide and varied as human need. In this way he gave the people an opportunity of translating their aroused religious impulses into deeds. Once he took a collection to help repair damage done by a fire at Harvard College. In February, 1760, he collected £400 sterling which was sent to Dr. Francke at Halle through Dr. Ziegenhagen, the Court preacher of King George of England, to be distributed to the needy among the Lutherans and German Reformed people.[7] The next year he raised the same amount for the same purpose. All the time he was providing funds for the Bethesda Orphanage in Georgia. Numerous money-raising deputations from the Colonies sought his help, for

---

[7] *The Journal of Henry Melchior Muhlenberg*, 3 vols. Translated by Theodore G. Tappert and John W. Doberstein (Philadelphia, 1942), I, 703.

he was in touch with all the benevolently minded people
in the three kingdoms. Thus he assisted Samuel Davies
and Gilbert Tennent when they came seeking funds for
the College of New Jersey; as he did also for Nathaniel
Whitaker and Samson Occom who came to raise funds for
Moore's Indian Charity School, which, as a result of the
astonishing success of the enterprise, led to the founding
of Dartmouth College.

To use Bishop McConnell's words, Whitefield was always valiantly and eloquently "on the side of the more
genuine humanity." [8] Some of those who have written of
Whitefield and his work in recent times have called attention to the fact that he possessed a very ordinary intellect,
and assume that they have thus discredited his whole work
and influence. But they overlook "that it was a profusion of
qualities other than the strictly intellectual which helped
to keep religion close to human life in eighteenth-century
America."

III

Of the several phases of the great colonial revivals the
southern was the most significant from the standpoint of
forging new religious forces and setting the pattern for a
new type of religious activity. The Middle Colony revival
put new life and energy into the Dutch Reformed and
Presbyterian Churches, particularly, but as a whole the old
religious patterns remained dominant. This is shown by
the fact that the schism in Presbyterianism, caused by the
revival which occurred in 1745, was healed in 1758 by the

---

[8] McConnell, *op. cit.*, 99–100.

reunion of the Old and New Side groups, and thereafter Presbyterianism settled down into the usual and accepted Presbyterian procedures and methods. The same thing is true of the effect of the New England awakenings. Congregationalism was reinvigorated, but to a large degree it remained the old Congregationalism of the former century, as far as methods of carrying on religious activities were concerned. This helps to account for the failure of Congregationalism to meet the demands of the new nation following independence; it was entirely too self-satisfied with its past to seek new ways of doing things.

The southern awakenings, on the other hand, left the religious situation in Maryland, Virginia, and the Carolinas radically different than it had been previously. The Congregational Church was the dominant religious body in New England before the revivals; it was still dominant at the end, although rifts had taken place in it. The same was true of the Middle Colony situation. But in the Southern Colonies, new religious forces arose out of the revivals which not only were to change the religious complexion of Maryland and Virginia, the principal strongholds of colonial Anglicanism, but eventually of the entire nation itself. Out of the southern revivals came something new and aggressive and distinctively American. This new religious aggressiveness is best represented by the separate or revivalistic Baptists and the Methodists. It was out of this background that both started on their amazing growth and development.

The southern awakenings were started by Presbyterians from the Middle Colonies. Some Log College evangelists, traveling in Virginia, came in contact with a religious movement that had been begun in Hanover County by some laymen meeting together to read religious books. Out of this came the Hanover or Virginia revival which, under the dynamic leadership of Samuel Davies—himself a graduate of Samuel Blair's Log College in Pennsylvania—became an increasingly important force in Virginia. The Hanover Presbytery, formed in 1755 with Davies as the first moderator, marks the beginning of the long line of southern Presbyteries, which came to be seed plots of frontier cultural influence of great significance.

Perhaps the most distinctive contribution of the Presbyterians in the southern revivals was that they helped clear the field for the more aggressive Baptists and Methodists. When the revivalistic Presbyterians began their work in Virginia the status of dissenters was, to say the least, in confusion, and the Presbyterians met bitter opposition from the Established clergy as well as from the colonial officials. The question as to whether the Toleration Act passed by the British Parliament in 1689 applied to Virginia had not been determined, and was raised again and again in the early days of Samuel Davies' ministry in Virginia. Under Davies' leadership this question was definitely answered in favor of the dissenters. In fact, Davies himself, acting as his own attorney, successfully argued the question before the General Court, with the Attorney General, Peyton Randolph, as his opponent, and won a favorable decision.[1]

---

[1] George H. Bost, *Samuel Davies: Colonial Revivalist and Champion of Religious Toleration* (Typed Ph.D. thesis; Chicago, 1942), 182 ff.

Though starting a religious movement whose influence has persisted to this day, the Virginia Presbyterians with their elaborate creedal demands and their tradition of an educated ministry hardly touched the great mass of the plain people. In fact, Presbyterianism has never become a strong body in the south.

The next phase of the southern revival, the Baptist, differed widely from the Presbyterian. It began under the leadership of two New Englanders, Shubael Stearns and Daniel Marshall, who had come out of the Separate Baptist movement; a movement directly related to the New England revival and which brought division to many New England Congregational churches. Neither Stearns nor Marshall had been educated for the ministry, and both came into the south as farmer-preachers. Finally settling just over the southern Virginia boundary in North Carolina, then a frontier, they began to evangelize throughout all the region. As their work continued other farmer-preachers were "raised up," who in turn carried on their work in ever-widening itineraries. They gave particular attention to neglected neighborhoods, to frontier communities, and to humble people. In their preaching they appealed to the emotions primarily, with the result that there were many excesses. So great were the crowds which attended their meetings that they were compelled to preach out of doors. At one such meeting an eyewitness saw:

multitudes, some roaring on the ground, some wringing their hands, some in extacies, some praying, some weeping; and others so outrageously cursing and swearing that it was thought they were really possessed of the devil.

Some of their preachers, as John Waller and Samuel Harris, gained widespread reputations and people came for miles to attend their meetings. The long list of men who gave themselves to this kind of work without compensation of any kind, other than that which comes from an easy conscience, is, to say the least, astonishing.[2] As a result of this widespread effort to reach the humble and poor with the softening influence of the gospel, the growth of the Separate or revivalistic Baptists throughout North Carolina and Virginia was phenomenal.

Since the Baptists held as their cardinal principle the separation of Church and State and complete religious liberty, they gave little or no heed to the requirements in Virginia to secure licenses for their meeting houses and ministers. As a consequence, persecution fell upon them. The fact also that they were generally humble people and their meetings often attended with emotional extravagances aroused disgust and contempt among the so-called "upper classes." One of the charges made against the Baptist preachers was that they were disturbers of the peace and were responsible for calling unlawful assemblies which took people away from the farms and plantations, and encouraged "habits of idleness and neglect of their necessary business." These are the same charges which were brought

---

[2] James B. Taylor, *Virginia Baptist Ministers*, 2 vols. (New York, 1860), contains the biographies of 228 preachers, most of them of the farmer-preacher type.

against the New England revivalists on the part of the representatives of the "standing order," an indication that the privileged classes were fearful of losing their privileges as a consequence of the religious revolution under way.

The coming of Methodism into the American colonies constitutes the third and last phase of the colonial revivals. Until very recent years Methodist historians have thought of their beginnings in America as an isolated movement, owing little if anything to contemporary influences. But, as a matter of fact, the great colonial awakening which had swept over the colonies from 1725 to 1770 prepared the soil for the Methodist seed. Another fact which needs emphasis in regard to the beginnings of American Methodists is that their first real foothold was obtained in Virginia and that it came about as a result of the influence exerted by an evangelical Anglican clergyman, Devereux Jarratt, who owed his conversion to the Presbyterians.

From the very beginning Methodism's emphasis in religion was individualistic. John Wesley held that religion was a personal matter; his appeal was for "individual, concrete experience," and his sermons were so effectual because they were addressed directly to men and women. He had no use, however, for extreme quietism and would have nothing of "solitary religion." He once stated that "the gospel of Christ knows no religion but social; no holiness but social holiness." [3] Wesley, however, sought to "combine the qualities of an individualistic, intense reli-

---

[3] Umphrey Lee, *John Wesley and Modern Religion* (Nashville, 1936), especially chapter xi, "Individualism and Emotion in Religion."

gious piety . . . with those qualities characteristic of the Church." [4] He expected the Methodist movement to remain within the Anglican Church, not only in England but also in America.[5]

IV

In this rapid survey of colonial Revivalism I have attempted to show that, from New England on the north to Georgia on the south, the revivalists stressed individualistic religion. The emphasis everywhere was upon man's personal needs; every man was expected to find his own way to God. In a pioneer society this emphasis was both natural and inevitable, for a pioneer society is a self-reliant individualistic society. Under such conditions even the legalistic theology of Calvin became in the hands of the colonial preachers a personalized theology meeting personal needs and searching out the hearts of individuals. All this implied the right of each individual to have his own religious experience, which did not need to be like any other. The emphasis upon the individual therefore meant variability; implied in it is the right to be different. And is this not basic in democracy; the right of the individual to live his

---

[4] *Ibid.*

[5] The early Virginia Methodists considered themselves as Church of England people. An interesting entry in the Journal of Edward Dromgoole for July 10, 1779, bears out this fact: "I was greatly mortified in class meeting to find such deadness among the members and I found afterwards that they frequently neglect their own meetings and go to hear Dissenters whch seldom fails to make Christians doubtful and no wonder when they hear such doctrines as predestination and final perseverance and believers baptism." From the *Dromgoole Papers* (University of North Carolina).

own life; his right to life, liberty, and the pursuit of happiness?[1]

The revivalists placed stress on the doctrine that all men are equal in the sight of God. When this doctrine is preached to humble people, it inevitably develops self-respect and a desire to have a part in the management of their own affairs. The preachers of the Great Awakening sought to reach all classes of men; slaves as well as masters; poor as well as rich; ignorant as well as learned. They knew no social distinctions. To them all were on the same plane; all were sinners and in need of a Saviour, whose grace alone availed. Thus the revivals were a great leveling force in American colonial society; they sowed the basic seeds of democracy more widely than any other single influence.

For the first time in colonial America, the common people found a leadership from among their own numbers. This was true everywhere, but particularly true among the Presbyterians, Baptists, and Methodists. Their preachers were men of their own kind, most of them from the humbler walks of life. They were in most instances, it is true, uneducated as far as the schools were concerned, but in native ability it would be difficult to find among any any other class of men of their time the equal of Samuel Harris, John Leland, George Shadford, Philip Gatch, and a long list of others. Through their leadership, and that of

---

[1] For an excellent summary of the influence of the colonial revival on the growth of democracy see W. M. Gewehr's *The Great Awakening in Virginia* (Durham, N. C., 1930), chapter viii, "Contributions to the Rise of Democracy."

others like them, the great mass of the plain people came to a realization of their own importance as well as their own strength.

Among the democratic influences coming out of the revivals was the great increase in the number of congregations which had popular forms of church government. Baptist congregational government is a pure democracy, and men who had never before had a voice in government of any kind found themselves, as members of a Baptist congregation, with an equal voice in managing the affairs of the church. The Methodist form of organization, though highly centralized and authoritarian, nevertheless gave full right of self-expression to every member, women as well as men, in the Class meetings. Not only was this his or her right, it was a duty; and, as a matter of fact, no religious body placed greater stress upon the activity of individuals than did the Methodist. This, as has already been pointed out, is the real essence of democracy. The Presbyterians, also, though nominally tied to the Church of Scotland in the colonial period, were in practice a self-governing body. Presbyteries like that of Hanover in Virginia managed their own affairs with little or no outside influence.

As the colonial period drew to its close and the War for Independence approached, these new revivalistic groups gave increasing evidence of their consciousness of their political strength. The Baptists, particularly, took the lead in the agitation for equal rights for all religious bodies. In Virginia they were responsible for a great flood of petitions making this demand. A Baptist petition of 1784 reads:

"We do not ask this, Gentlemen, as a favour which you have a privilege either to grant or withhold at pleasure, but as what we have a just claim to as freemen of the Commonwealth." [2] The Presbyterians were also demanding equal rights for all denominations, "not as a pittance of courtesy, but . . . as their patrimony which cannot be withheld without flagrant fraud, pride, and injustice. . ." The Hanover Presbytery made certain definite demands upon government that their meetings be protected as adequately as were those of the Establishment; that they have freedom in speaking and writing upon all religious subjects; that they have the right to hold property for the support of their churches and schools; and the full right to enjoy the free exercise of their religion "without molestation or danger of incurring any penalty whatsoever." The petition ends with: "We are petitioning in favor of a church that is neither contemptible nor obscure." [3]

Virginia could not have played her conspicuous part in the movement for the independence of America if there had not been present within her borders a large dissenting element, created by the revivals, favorable to the principles of the revolution. Not only was this true of Virginia but everywhere the revivalistic bodies which had been greatly increased by the revivals, took almost unanimously the side of the party demanding all the rights of free men. [4]

---

[2] Numerous MSS. petitions may be found in the Archives of the Virginia State Library.
[3] Gewehr, *op. cit.*, 203.
[4] C. H. Maxson, *The Great Awakening in the Middle Colonies* (Chicago, 1920), 150.

CHAPTER THREE

THEODORE J. FRELINGHUYSEN AND THE LOG COLLEGE EVANGELISTS

COLONIAL REVIVALISTS naturally fall into three more or less distinct groups. The first are the Presbyterian Log College revivalists, whose work, though largely confined to the Middle Colonies, extended into Virginia and North Carolina. These were the graduates of William Tennent's Log College at Neshaminy, Pennsylvania, and the other Log Colleges which arose in succeeding years, such as that at Fagg's Manor in Pennsylvania and at Nottingham, in Maryland. The second group are the college-trained revivalists, found mostly among New England Congregationalists, though some, like Jonathan Dickinson and Aaron Burr, found their way into the Presbyterian fold. A third group, set apart by their lack of formal education, are the Baptist farmer-preachers, particularly those in Virginia and North Carolina, and the early Methodist missionaries and lay preachers sent over by John Wesley, and their native American co-laborers.

Though differing in their background and training, as well as in their theological positions and ecclesiastical affiliations, all three of these groups of colonial revivalists had one supreme common concern—the bringing of people to repentance and to a conversion experience. To this one end all their preaching was pointed. Much of colonial revivalistic preaching was extemporaneous and only a few of these sermons have come down to us in the form of

44

notes taken by hearers. For a study of colonial revivalistic preaching, therefore, we are dependent upon the relatively few revival sermons that found their way into print. These were naturally the sermons of the educated revivalists, and for that reason they must furnish the principal material for this survey.

I

Chronologically, Theodore Jacobus Frelinghuysen should be treated first, since it is through his activities in central New Jersey that the colonial awakenings began. Though born in Germany, near the Dutch border, the son of a Reformed minister, he learned the Dutch language and entered the Dutch Reformed Church. Educated largely by his father, from the start he identified himself with the evangelical party, and throughout his life was noted for his revivalistic zeal almost to a fanatical degree. His insistence upon inner religion was greatly increased on coming to the pastorate of three new Dutch Reformed congregations in the Raritan Valley in central New Jersey. These were relatively new communities and religion was at low ebb among the rude Dutch farmers of the region. Young Frelinghuysen had welcomed the opportunity of coming to America, for there he would be free from the restraint of the Old World conservatism, and would be able to carry on such a religious reformation as would have been impossible in Holland.

Young in years—he was twenty-nine when he came to America—Dominie Frelinghuysen set about his work with energy and courage. The Dutch had not come to America

as a consequence of religious persecution, so they had not
been alienated from the institutions and ways of their old
European home. The thing they desired most of all religiously was to preserve their Dutch nationality and the old
ways of carrying on their church. This was at the opposite
pole from young Dominie Frelinghuysen's idea. As a consequence it was not long before there was open conflict,
and a party of opposition arose not only among his parishioners but also among the Dutch clergy, particularly in
New York, the stronghold of the Dutch Reformed Church
in America.

In his very first sermon in his new parish Dominie Frelinghuysen attacked the general laxity of the congregation.
"The outward performance of religious duties," he stated,
"without a suitable frame of mind, He [the Lord] hates."
He appealed to them to "lay aside all pride, haughtiness,
and ideas of inherent worthliness, and humble themselves
before the Lord; and to confess and acknowledge themselves to be dust and ashes." [1] This was shock number one
to the self-satisfied Dutch Calvinists, but it was only the
beginning of a whole series of shocks which they were to
receive in short order from their youthful minister. When
the first communion time came he announced that only the
"penitent, believing, upright and converted persons" were
to be invited to the Lord's table. His idea of the Sacrament
and its purpose he set forth in an early sermon, as follows:

---

[1] Theodore Jacobus Frelinghuysen, *Sermons,* translated from the Dutch
and prefaced by a sketch of the author's life by Rev. William Demarest
(New York, 1856), 26 ff.

We also have a sanctuary under the New Testament—the Lord's supper, which has come in place of the Passover, and which, it is explicitly and solemnly declared, that none of the unconverted, who are still in their natural and unclean state, because not sanctified by the Holy Ghost, should approach this sanctuary, and partake of these holy things. He has at the same time enjoined upon the overseers of the church, that they debar strangers and the ungodly, and put them from among them; that the covenant of God may not be profaned, and his wrath stirred up against the whole congregation, and the Lord remove from his blessing spirit and grace from his church.

. . . For whom is the Lord's supper instituted? It is not instituted for the dead; for they are already in their place, where they shall remain forever. It must also not be administered to the dying, for they are not in a state to receive it; nor to children, because (they are) unable to examine themselves, but to living adults; yet not to all who are partakers of corporeal life; since it is instituted only for the regenerated, who are possessed of spiritual food that spiritual men only can partake of, to their invigoration.[2]

On the occasion of his administering the Lord's supper for the fourth time, he stated from the pulpit:

Truly, it is manifest that the Lord's supper is now frequently thus desecrated; for not only does one unworthy approach; but how many of those who receive the sacred elements are either ignorant, or ungodly; as drunkards, slanderers, backbiters, profaners of God's name and day, vain and worldly minded,

---

[2] *Ibid.*, 53.

or merely moral persons who do not possess, but hate true godliness! . . . I have three times (it is now the fourth time)
administered the Lord's supper and urged this point, that the
unconverted may not approach, and the wicked must, according to our doctrine, be debarred. But what murmuring has this
excited. How many tongues set on fire of hell, have uttered
their slanders? . . . I would ask you, who have been, and
perhaps still are so greatly displeased on this account, Is not
this the doctrine of the Reformed Church? . . . Why then
disobey the truth? Why make yourselves guilty of such
slanders and backbitings? Say you that I speak too hard and
sharply? Must I not speak in accordance with the word of
God?[3]

On one occasion while administering the Lord's supper
the young dominie remarked: "See! See! Even the people
of the world and the impenitent are coming, that they may
eat and drink judgment to themselves." This remark
caused some of the people who had left their seats to
commune to stop and turn back, "not daring to commune."[4]

In his preaching Frelinghuysen continually stressed the
necessity of a personal religious experience. He bore down
constantly upon a change of heart as an essential for Christian living, and all his energies were directed toward helping his people secure such a personal experience. This end,
however, the young dominie did not always pursue gently.
Perhaps, he believed that it was only stern denunciation

[3] *Ibid.,* 65–66.
[4] Abraham Messler, *Memorial Sermons and Historical Notes* (New
York, 1873), 170.

that would avail to move some of his hardened parishioners, which accounts for the following fear-producing harangue:

Come hither, ye careless, at ease in sin, ye carnal and earthly minded, ye unchaste whoremongers, adulterers, ye proud, haughty men and women, ye devotees of pleasure, drunkards, gamblers, ye disobedient, ye wicked rejectors of the Gospel, ye hypocrites and dissemblers, how suppose ye it will go with you? The period of grace is concluded. All earthly satisfaction ceaseth. Your agonies and pains as to soul and body have no end, for ye shall be cast into that lake which burns with fire and brimstone, where is weeping and gnashing of teeth, where the smoke of their torment ascendeth forever, where your worm dieth not and your fire is not quenched . . .

. . . Be filled with terror, ye impure swine, adulterers and whoremongers, and consider that without true repentance, ye shall soon be with the impure devils; for I announce a fire hotter than that of Sodom and Gomorrah to all that burn in their lusts.[5]

Such preaching gained two kinds of response. One was resentment and bitter opposition; the other sincere repentance and conversion. Some of the Dutch ministers were scandalized and were soon organized to resist Frelinghuysen's crusade. Dominie Boel of New York was the ringleader of the opposition and visited Frelinghuysen's congregations to secure evidence against him.[6] His preaching was pronounced heretical and his removal through the

[5] Frelinghuysen, *op. cit.*, 311–314.
[6] The whole story of this conflict may be read in the Documents printed in the *Ecclesiastical Records of the State of New York* (Albany, 1902), scattered reference (see Index volume), III, IV.

courts was attempted; an appeal was even made to the Governor to remove the heretic, but without success. To cap the climax there was published in 1725 a volume of 150 pages called the *Klagte* (Complaint),[7] a contemptible piece of ministerial skulduggery, to which some of Frelinghuysen's friends in the ministry felt compelled to reply. For years the unseemly warfare continued, and the issues involved divided practically every Dutch congregation in America, and was finally referred to the Classis of Amsterdam. Such were some of the unfortunate results of Dominie Frelinghuysen's brave stand. The good results, however, far outweighed the bad. Gradually his straightforward preaching brought results. At first the young people and the poor began to respond, and by 1726 the dry bones began to stir. Even the deacons and elders were converted and the congregations in his four churches began to increase, and by the following year a great revival was sweeping through the whole region. Frelinghuysen was called upon to visit other churches, and in a few instances he invaded other minister's parishes uninvited. But as a whole he kept within the bounds of good ministerial order, and before the end of his life, which came in 1748, he had triumphed over his enemies and his latter years were blessed with peace and well-deserved honor.

Theodore J. Frelinghuysen was very evidently a preacher of dramatic power. He had a penchant for arresting topics; within a year after his arrival he published four sermons, entitled, "The Poor and Contrite," "God's Temple," "The

---

[7] For all the documents relating to the *Complaint*, see *ibid.*, 2244 ff.

Acceptable Communicant," and "The Church's Duty to
Her Members." An especially searching sermon published
in April 1729 was on the subject, "A Mirror that does not
Flatter"; in the autumn of the same year another sermon
appeared on the subject, "If the Righteous scarcely be
saved, where shall the ungodly and the sinner appear?"
In 1733, Frelinghuysen published a volume of ten sermons. In the Preface he states:

He [the author] is not ignorant how classic is the present
age; and he is not writing for the learned, but for the plain,
and the unlettered. It shall suffice him if he express himself
according to the style of the Holy Spirit, in a clear and simple
manner, and so that he can be understood by all.

In the *Dictionary of American Biography* there are biographical sketches of three other Frelinghuysens besides
the founder of the family in America, all of whom are the
direct descendants of Theodore Jacobus. Frelinghuysen
married an American wife, the daughter of a well-to-do
Dutch farmer. Her two daughters became ministers' wives
and her five sons all became ministers. Thus the Frelinghuysen influence lived on in the Dutch Reformed Church
under the Frelinghuysen name, and it has continued to
do so to this day. Frelinghuysen became a tireless advocate of an American-trained ministry and urged the establishment of a college and theological seminary to that end.
He also stood for self-government of the Dutch Churches
in America, and depreciated the continual interference of
the Classis of Amsterdam with American affairs. In other

words, his was an Americanizing influence of great significance, and the things for which he stood came finally to fruition in Queens College and in the New Brunswick Theological Seminary.[8]

II

As has already been noted (see Chapter II), Frelinghuysen and his co-laborers helped prepared the way for the Scotch-Irish revival which followed upon the heels of the Dutch awakening in central New Jersey. In the very region where Frelinghuysen's churches were located, a new Scotch-Irish population was pushing in, and to them in the autumn 1727 came Reverend Gilbert Tennent to serve as their minister. Some of the Dutch people opposed to Frelinghuysen had signed the call, hoping evidently that the coming of an English Presbyterian to the region would embarrass him. Other Dutch Reformed people, supporters of Frelinghuysen, also signed the call, because they were sincerely desirous of bringing religion to their English neighbors, many of whom they considered as "sheep gone astray."

In a letter from the Consistory of the Churches on the Raritan, signed by Frelinghuysen and four other ministers, dated October 2, 1731, addressed to the Classis of Amsterdam defending the part played by the Dutch Reformed people in the coming of Gilbert Tennent to the region, occurs this statement:

---

[8] An excellent treatment of Theodore J. Frelinghuysen in connection with the colonial awakening is found in C. H. Maxson, *The Great Awakening in the Middle Colonies* (Chicago, 1916), chapter ii, "Frelinghuysen and the Beginning of the Revival Among the Dutch Reformed."

Rev. [Gilbert] Tennent is a Presbyterian, and they are surely orthodox. And ought we to oppose and persecute English Presbyterians in an English country. God preserve us from doing so! For have they not, even in England and Ireland, freedom of conscience and of worship? That some of our adherents attend his services and help support him, we neither can, nor ought to, forbid.[1]

The coming of Gilbert Tennent to New Brunswick marks the beginning of the Presbyterian phase of the colonial revivals. He cannot be understood, however, apart from what may be called the "Log College group." This group was composed of the elder Tennent, William, Sr., Gilbert, his eldest son, and Gilbert's three younger brothers, William, Jr., John and Charles, the two Blair brothers, Samuel and John, Samuel Finley, William Robinson and John Rowland. To these also must be added at least one other name, Samuel Davies, in many respects the most able and distinguished of them all.

Little is known of the intimate life of the senior Tennent. A native of Ireland, a graduate of the University of Edinburgh (1695), he married in 1702 a daughter of Gilbert Kennedy, a Presbyterian clergyman residing in County Down, Ireland, and to whom were born the four sons mentioned above, and a daughter. The Tennents came to America in 1716; the father, although ordained as a priest in the Church of Ireland, had never secured a church there—one of the principal reasons, probably, why

----

[1] See Letter addressed to the Classis of Amsterdam, by the Consistory of the United Churches of Raritan, October 2, 1731. *Ecclesiastical Records of the State of New York*, op. cit., 2556-57.

he decided to become a Presbyterian on reaching America. Between the time of his arrival in America to 1726 he served three short pastorates, when he was called to minister to the Presbyterian Church at Neshaminy, in Bucks County, Pennsylvania, located some twenty miles north of Philadelphia. Here he continued to his death in 1746. His significance is not due to his preaching, but to the fact that he conducted a school in a log building (erected 1736) near his home, where in the course of twenty years as remarkable and talented a group of young men as ever entered the Christian ministry in America received their training and inspiration. This group of young men, "the graduates" of William Tennent's "Log College," completely changed the course of American Presbyterians. If a teacher is to be judged by his students, William Tennent, Sr., must be ranked among the greatest of America's teachers.[2]

The only contemporary description of Tennent's Log College that has come down to us is that found in George Whitefield's *Journal*. Whitefield visited Neshaminy in the autumn of 1739.

"The place," he states, "wherein the young men study now is in contempt called *The College*. It is a log house, about twenty feet long and near as many broad; and to me it seemed to resemble the school of the old prophets, for their habitations

---

[2] William Tennent's farm of 100 acres, on which the Log College was located, lay on the road between Philadelphia and New York. For an appraisal of Tennent as a teacher see Maxson, *The Great Awakening in the Middle Colonies*, chapter iii, "The Tennents and the Beginnings of the Revival Among the Presbyterians."

were mean; and that they sought not great things for themselves is plain from those passages of Scripture, wherein we
are told that each of them took them a beam to build them a
house. . . . All that we can say of most of our universities is,
they are glorious without. From this despised place, seven or
eight worthy ministers of Jesus have lately been sent forth;
more are almost ready to be sent, and the foundation is now
laying for the instruction of many others."

Frelinghuysen's friendliness for the young Presbyterian
minister, Gilbert Tennent, doubtless strengthened the
younger man's revivalistic tendencies. As a result he was
soon emphasizing the same cardinal evangelical doctrines
in his preaching that had marked the preaching of Frelinghuysen, and New Brunswick became the center of an
expanding revivalistic excitement among the people of
Presbyterian background. George Whitefield was greatly
impressed by Gilbert Tennent's preaching. After hearing
him preach for the first time in New York in 1738 he declared him a "son of thunder" who does not regard "the
face of man." "Hypocrites must either soon be converted
or enraged at his preaching." Whitefield's prophesy as to
the effects of Tennent's preaching was soon fulfilled, for,
to use the words of Thomas Prince in his *Christian History*
describing Tennent's evangelistic tour of New England in
1740, "multitudes were awakened" in Charlestown, and
even in Cambridge, both in town and college, "the shaking
among the dry bones was general, and several of the students have received consolation." On the other hand none
of the revivalists, unless it was George Whitefield, was

more denounced by the opposers of the revival than was Gilbert Tennent. In his early years, particularly, he went beyond all others in his denunciation of those whose religion was merely formal and outward. Incapable of fear, and with a burning zeal for what he believed to be true religion, and with strident voice and powerful delivery, he was soon recognized as the principal Presbyterian revivalist.

Gilbert Tennent's early preaching was largely extemporaneous. His first published sermon appeared in 1735 entitled "Solemn Warning to the Secure World, from the God of Terrible Majesty; or the Presumptuous Sinner Detected, His Pleas Considered, and His Doom Displayed." His most widely heralded sermon was preached at Nottingham, Maryland, on the subject "The Dangers of an Unconverted Ministry," which was a terrible blast at all those ministers who opposed the revival. It pictured the majority of ministers as "plastered hypocrites, having the form of godliness, but not its powers." He characterized as "moral negroes" those who hinder instead of help others "in at the strait gate"; he likened them to caterpillars who "labour to devour every green thing," and declared that they resembled the Pharisees of Christ's day "as one crow does another." He expected this sermon would arouse a hornet's nest, and he was not mistaken. It did the cause of revivalism far more harm than good, and before long he became humbly apologetic for it, as well as for other harsh denunciations of like nature in which he indulged.

Gilbert Tennent's leadership more than any other single factor was responsible for the division in colonial Presbyterianism which occurred in 1741, when the Synod of Philadelphia expelled the New Brunswick Presbytery made up mostly of the Log College graduates. Two years later he was called to the pastorate of the Second Presbyterian Church of Philadelphia which was being formed by George Whitefield's converts in that city. On coming to the Philadelphia pulpit Gilbert Tennent began to write his sermons and thereafter preached from a manuscript, thereby limiting his vivacity and natural eloquence. The principal emphasis in his preaching, however, remained revivalistic, as is illustrated by the following sermon preached during his first year in Philadelphia.

The text is Jeremiah 10:10:

But the Lord is the true God, he is the living God, and an everlasting king: at his wrath the earth shall tremble, and the nations shall not be able to abide his indignation.

After explaining the text, he proceeds to prove the life and reality of God. Then follows a discussion of the nature of the divine life and the relation of the divine life to our life; while the last main heading is "An Alarm to the Sinner," a part of which follows:

Finally, the consideration of the Life of God should incline us to live in him; which consists principally in the following particulars, viz., (1) in directing all our actions, whether Natural, Civil, or Religious, to his glory as our highest work; (2) in conforming our actions according to his revealed will; (3) it consists in living by the power of God. He is the author of our life; His is our life, yea has died that we might live; not to ourselves but to him that has died for us.

   .   .   .   .   .   .

O! therefore while we do live, let us live to the glory of God, and labor to be fervent and lively in his service.

His closing appeal is for sinners to AWAKE.

I beseech you, Friends, by all the happiness of heaven, by all the torments of hell, for the sake of God, the Father, Son and Spirit by all the regard you owe to your deathless souls, your reason, your conscience, as well as the ambassadors of Christ among you, that ye *awake*. I beseech you as a messenger of the great God, as on my bended knees, by the groans, tears, and wounds of Christ that ye would *Awake*. Yea, I charge you all by the curses of the law, and blessings of the gospels, that ye would *Awake*. My friends, you are witnesses against yourselves, that I have set Death and Life before you; O choose Life that ye may live. *Let the wicked man forsake his way, and the unrighteous man his thoughts, and turn to God and he will have mercy upon him, and to our God for he will abundantly pardon!* O Sirs! consider these things, as ye would answer at the Tribunal of Christ on the last day.[3]

While to Gilbert Tennent belongs a large share of the blame for dividing colonial Presbyterianism in 1741, he deserves a major part of the credit for healing the division. The following extracts from a letter he wrote to Jonathan

---

[3] This extract is taken from Sermon XXI, in *Twenty-three Sermons Upon the Chief End of Man . . . Preached in Philadelphia Anno Dom. 1743. By Gilbert Tennent* (Philadelphia, 1744).

Dickinson, in February 1741 or 1742, depict a contrite and chastened Gilbert Tennent.

I have had many afflicting thoughts about the debates that have subsisted for some time in our Synod: I would to God the breach were healed, if it was the will of the Almighty. As for my own part, wherein I have mismanaged in doing what I did:—I do look upon it to be my duty, and should be willing to acknowledge it in the openest manner. I cannot justify the excessive heat of temper which has sometimes appeared in my conduct. I have been of late (since I returned from New England) visited with much spiritual dissertations, temptations, and distresses of various kinds, coming in a thick and almost continual succession, which have given me a greater discovery of myself than I think I ever had before. . . .

Here follow a few sentences in regard to the excesses of the Moravians with whom he has had some controversy, which has evidently brought home to him the harm to religion resulting when people of sound principles quarrel among themselves, which he sees only gives such "fanatics" a chance to increase. The letter closes with:

Alas for it! my soul is sick of these things: I wish that some scriptural healing methods could be fallen upon to put an end to these confusions.

Then follows a long postscript dealing with James Davenport's conduct. Particularly strong is his condemnation of "The practice of openly exposing ministers, who are supposed to be unconverted in public discources"; this, he says, "serves only to provoke them, (instead of doing

them any good) and to declare our own arrogance."
Strange words coming from the man who but three years
before had preached on "The Danger of an Unconverted
Ministry"! Another practice he condemns is "the sending
out of unlearned men to teach others, upon the supposi-
tion of their piety." This, he says, "seems to bring the ministry into contempt; to cherish enthusiasms, and bring all
into confusion." "The Practice of singing in the streets,"
he thinks, "is a piece of weakness and enthusiastical Osten-
tation." [4]

In 1749 Gilbert Tennent published his *Irenicum Eccle-
siasticum*, or *A Humble, Impartial Essay upon the Peace
of Jerusalem.* By this time the revival enthusiasm had
cooled and both the Old Side as well as the New Side
Synods were willing to make concessions. The result was
the formation in 1758 of the Synod of New York and
Philadelphia which happily united the former opposing
bodies.

One of his biographers thus summarizes Gilbert Tennent as a preacher:

As a preacher he was equalled by few; his reasoning was
strong, his language forcible and often sublime; his manner
warm and earnest. Most pungent were his addresses to the
conscience. With admirable dexterity he exposed the false
hope of the hypocrite, and searched the corrupt heart to the
bottom.

.   .   .   .

---

[4] This letter was published in the *Boston Evening Post*, July 26, 1742.

He was a mark for many archers. They emptied their quivers on him; he was sore wounded by their calumnies; but he "shook off the venomous beasts," and lived, serving Christ, approved of God and acceptable to men.[5]

Among the other Log College graduates John Rowland is outstanding as a revivalist preacher. His licensing by the Presbytery of New Brunswick, contrary to the Synod's ruling that only graduates of recognized colleges should be received, gave notice to the Synod that the revivalists were determined to maintain their position. The Presbytery also recommended his acceptance of a call to two churches, Maidenhead and Hopewell, towns, which lay just outside their boundary. At first denied the use of the church buildings, Rowland preached in barns and so great were the crowds that he was compelled to use the largest barns available. For months he preached on but three themes—conviction, repentance, and conversion—and from the most arousing texts. Sunday evening meetings were introduced, something entirely new at that time. The effect of such preaching was extraordinary and large numbers were brought under conviction. Then suddenly the preacher changed his emphasis. He now began to use "inviting and

---

[5] Richard Webster, *A History of the Presbyterian Church in America, from Its Origin, Until the Year* 1760. With biographical sketches of its early ministers (Philadelphia, 1857). Biographical sketch of Gilbert Tennent, 387–397. The most extended account of Gilbert Tennent is Archibald Alexander, *Biographical Sketches of the Founder and Principal Alumni of the Log College. Together with an Account of the Revivals of Religion Under Their Ministry* (Philadelphia, 1851).

encouraging" subjects. His principal theme was now the infinite love and pity of God for sinful man. "The eye that had flashed with the anger of God" now became a well of tears. The result was a wave of conversions and an end to all controversy.[6]

The two brothers, Samuel and John Blair, after a period of revivalistic activity, devoted themselves primarily to education. Both were born in Ulster, Ireland; both sat at the feet of William Tennent; both were revivalist preachers of notable ability. After a short pastorate in New Jersey, Samuel Blair was called (1739) to the thriving Scotch-Irish community of Londonderry, Chester County, Pennsylvania. When he arrived on the scene, he tells us that, "religion lay, as it were, a-dying, and ready to expire its last breath of life in this part of the visible church." A neighboring minister, who had supplied his pulpit during his absence on a journey in March 1740, had preached on the text Luke 13:7. "Then said he unto the dresser of his vineyard, Behold, these three years I come seeking fruit on this fig tree, and find none: cut it down; why cumbereth it the ground?" It was this sermon of the visiting preacher that started one of the most sweeping religious upheavals in the Middle Colonies. It continued throughout the summer and spread widely. Blair's Sunday audiences were "vastly large" and there was scarcely a sermon preached that did not produce "manifest evidences of impressions on the

[6] John Rowland, *A Narrative of the Revival . . . in Hopewell, Amwell and Maidenhead . . . and New Providence* (Philadelphia, 1745), quoted in Maxson, *op. cit.*, 36–37.

hearers." Often some would be "overcome and fainting; others deeply sobbing, hardly able to contain; others crying in a most dolorous manner; many others more silently weeping." There appeared also some unusual bodily exercises.[7]

Blair tells us that the main emphasis of his preaching that summer was upon the awful condition of those who were "not in Christ, giving the marks and characters of such as were in that condition," and then pointing the way of recovery through faith in Christ.

After the excitement of the revival died down, Samuel Blair opened a school, similar to that of William Tennent's at Neshaminy, which he continued to conduct until his death in 1751 at the early age of thirty-nine. Among those who were educated at his school was John Rodgers, the first Moderator of the General Assembly of the Presbyterian Church in America and one of the outstanding ministerial leaders in Revolutionary America. Another graduate was Samuel Davies, fourth President of the College of New Jersey. On the death of Samuel Blair his brother John was called to succeed him and he continued the School until he was summoned to be Professor of Theology at the College of New Jersey, where he remained until John Witherspoon assumed the Presidency and Professorship of Theology in 1768.

When Samuel Davies heard of the death of Samuel Blair, under whom he had obtained most of his education,

[7] For a description of this revival see Samuel Blair's own account in Alexander, *Log College*, op. cit., 173–192.

he wrote an elegy dedicated to his former teacher, from
which the following lines are taken:

> Surviving remnant of the sacred tribe,
> Who knew the worth these plaintive lays describe
> Tennents, three worthies of immortal fame,
> Brethren, by office, birth, in heart and name.
> Finley, who full enjoyed the unbosomed friend;
> Rodgers, whose soul he like his own refined;
> When all attention, eager to admit
> The flowing knowledge, at his reverend feet
> Raptured we sat; and thou above the rest,
> Brother and image of the dear deceased.
> Surviving Blair! Oh, let spontaneous flow
> The floods of tributary grief you owe.
> And in your number—if so mean a name
> May the sad honour of chief mourner claim,
> Oh! may my filial tears more copious flow,
> And swell the tide of universal woe.
> Oh! Blair! whom all the tenderest names commend,
> My father, tutor, pastor, brother, friend!
> While distance, the sad privilege denies,
> O'er thy tomb, to vent my bursting eyes,
> The Muse erects—the sole return allowed—
> This humble monument of gratitude.

III

As has been noted (Chapter II) the Presbyterian phase
of the Virginia revival was tied to the Middle Colony
awakening through certain revivalist preachers who had
come down from the New Brunswick Presbytery. Of these

Samuel Davies [1] was by far the most important. He spent
ten years in Virginia (1748–1758), and in that period
organized the revivalistic Presbyterians into a cohesive
body, fought and won the battle for the rights of dissenters
in Virginia, and gained the reputation as a preacher of
intercolonial distinction. In fact a good case can be made
for naming him the outstanding preacher of Colonial
America. He has been called "the animating soul of the
whole dissenting interest in Virginia and North Carolina." [2]

When Samuel Davies arrived in Hanover, Virginia, in
1748, a young man of twenty-four, the status of dissenters
was, to say the least, uncertain. He was the only New Side,
or revivalistic Presbyterian minister in the colony, though
there were several Old Side ministers in the western counties. He was anxious to avoid friction with the Established
Church clergy and one of his first achievements was to
secure the application of the English Toleration Act of
1689 to Virginia. Under his preaching, the revival which
was already under way before his arrival continued. While
his work was centered at Hanover, he made preaching excursions into other counties, and his fame as a preacher
spread abroad. In a letter to the Bishop of London in 1752,
Commissary William Dawson gives direct testimony of
Davies' success in the following words:

---

[1] George H. Bost, *Samuel Davies: Colonial Revivalist and Champion
of Religious Toleration*, op. cit., especially chapter ii, "A New-Light
Preacher and the Great Awakening."

[2] V. L. Collins, *Princeton*, 58.

The Dissenters were but an inconsiderable number before the late arrival of certain teachers from the northern colonies. . . . But since Mr. Davies has been allowed to officiate in so many places . . . there has been a great defection from our religious assemblies. The generality of his followers, I believe, were born and bred in our communion.[3]

Unlike the revival elsewhere the Virginia phase of the Presbyterian awakening was largely free from extravagances and excessive emotionalism. Nor was there any bitterness engendered comparable to that between the revivalists and anti-revivalists in the Middle and New England colonies. This was largely due to the fact that Davies refused to exchange epithets with his opponents, nor did he stoop to name calling and harsh accusations. His weapons were logic, persuasion, and appeal. He was singularly tolerant and catholic-spirited for the time in which he lived, and subordinated the interests of his beloved Presbyterianism to the larger concerns of Christianity. Dr. Finley, his successor at Princeton, said of him in his funeral sermon:

It would hardly be expected that one as rigid with respect to his own faith and practice could be so generous and catholic in his sentiments of those who differed from him in both. . . . He considered the visible kingdom of Christ as extended beyond the boundaries of this or that particular denomination. . . . Hence he gloried more in being Christian than in being a Presbyterian, though he was the latter from principle.

In a sermon entitled "The Sacred Import of the Chris-

[3] Bost, *op. cit.*, 45, quoted from Perry, *Virginia Documents*, 384–385.

tian Name" from the text, "The Disciples were called Christians first at Antioch" (Acts 11:26), is this telling appeal:

My brethren, I would warn you against this wretched, mischievous spirit of party. . . . A Christian! A Christian! let that be your highest distinction; let that be the name which you labour to deserve. God forbid that my ministry should be the occasion of diverting your attention to anything else. But I am happy that I can appeal to yourselves, whether I have, during several years of ministry among you, labored to instil into you the principle of bigotry, and make you warm proselytes to a party; or whether it has not been the great object of my zeal to inculcate upon you the grand essentials of our holy religion, and to make you sincere practical Christians. Alas! my dear people, unless I succeed in this, I labour to very little purpose, though I should presbyterianize the whole colony.[4]

An excellent example of Davies' revivalistic preaching is the sermon entitled "The Nature and Necessity of True Repentance," on the text Acts 17:30: "And the times of this ignorance God winked at; but now commandeth all men every where to repent." The sermon was first preached at New Kent, Virginia, on May 22, 1757. All of Davies' sermons were carefully prepared, and the theme elaborately developed. After placing the text in its setting, he sets forth as his second heading repentance as a duty of all mankind, because it is "enjoined by our natural reason";

---

[4] Davies, *Sermons*, 4 vols. (London, 1815), I. Sermon XII. This is a magnificent sermon, which might well be preached today.

"strongly enforced by the Jewish religion"; while the Gospel "affords the strongest motives . . . and the best helps and advantages for repentance." Even infidels agree on the necessity of repentance and it is universally recognized as an essential in the religion of a sinner. In the next heading the preacher defines repentance, stating, "I shall endeavor, with the utmost plainness and faithfulness, to tell you what gospel repentance is, and help you to determine whether ever you have been the subject of it." "First," he states, "repentance extends to the heart as well as to the practice" . . . "every true penitent is a critic upon his own heart." Second, repentance is "a deep sense of the intrinsic evil of sin, and a hearty sorrow for it as done against God." Many think they "repent of sin who have no proper sorrow on account of sin against God, but only on account of the punishment it is like to bring upon themselves. It is not sin they hate, but hell." . . . "God will never accept of that repentance which has the punishment and not the crime for its object." Third, it must extend to all known sin; fourth, repentance always includes reformation; "and lastly, evangelical repentance implies a believing application to God for pardon, only through Jesus Christ." It is the peculiar work of the Holy Spirit to produce repentance.

The sermon closes with a telling exhortation, as follows:

Let me then in the first place publish the royal edict of the King of heaven in this assembly; *God commandeth all men to repent*; He commands you in various ways; commands you with the motions of His Spirit striving with you, and by the voice of your own consciences, which is the voice of God;

commands you by His providence, which He has sent to you for this end. He now commands you by my mouth; for while I speak what His word authorizes, it does not lose its efficacy; nor cease to be his word by passing through my lips. Remember, He commands *you*, He lays his authority upon you, to repent. You are not left to your discretion in the case. Dare you reject the known, express command of the Divine Majesty?

Dare you go home this day with this additional guilt upon you, of disobeying a known command of the supreme Lord of heaven and earth? Dare you provoke him to jealousy? Are you stronger than he? Can you harden yourselves against him, and yet prosper? I again proclaim it aloud in your hearing. The King of kings, my Master, has issued out his royal mandate, requiring you by these presents to repent upon pain of everlasting damnation. This day it is proclaimed in your ears, therefore, this day repent. If you refuse to repent, let this conviction follow you home, and perpetually haunt you, that you have this day, when you were met together under pretense of worshipping God, knowingly disobeyed the great gospel-command. And to this great God you must answer for your disobedience.

. . . .

The question is not, *shall I repent?* For that is beyond a doubt. But the question is "shall I repent now, when it may reform and save me; or shall I put it off to the eternal world when my repentance will be my punishment, and can answer no end but to torment me?" [5]

---

[5] Samuel Davies, *op. cit.*, III. Sermon XLIV, 21–38.

In 1759 Samuel Davies succeeded Jonathan Edwards as President of the College of New Jersey, and died three years later at the age of thirty-seven. After his death his sermons were published in numerous editions, and continued to enjoy a large reading for many years both in England as well as America. Among the many prolific eighteenth-century preachers, few if any can be read more profitably today than Samuel Davies.

CHAPTER FOUR

THE COLONIAL REVIVALIST-THEOLOGIANS; JONATHAN DICKINSON AND JONATHAN EDWARDS

As REPRESENTATIVES of the college-trained colonial revivalists I have chosen Jonathan Dickinson and Jonathan Edwards. Both were graduates of Yale College—Dickinson in 1706; Edwards in 1720. Both gained distinction as theologians as well as revivalists; both were defenders of Calvinism and both introduced into their Calvinism a personal emphasis which gave to their preaching an emotional appeal. Both wrote defending the Great Awakening, and both serve to refute the notion, especially current in recent times, that only the ignorant and uneducated ministers were advocates of revivalism and only the emotionally unstable have stressed the place of feeling in religion. Both started their ministerial careers as Congregationalists and both ended their lives as Presidents of the College of New Jersey and within the fold of Presbyterianism. The famous Dr. John Erskine of Edinburgh is responsible for the statement "that the British Isles had produced no such writers on Divinity in the eighteenth century as Dickinson and Edwards."

From the middle of the seventeenth century there was a considerable movement of population southward from New England into the Middle Colonies, especially into New Jersey and along the north shore of Long Island.

Some were attracted by the broad meadows along the rivers flowing into New York harbor, promising better pasture for their flocks and herds, in contrast with the growing scarcity of pasture in eastern New England. Others, Quakers and Baptists, came to escape persecution at the hands of intolerant Massachusetts. Some, as the founders of Newark, New Jersey, came because of dissatisfaction over the Half-Way Covenant, where they hoped to found a "New Ark" in which the purity of their Church might not be contaminated. By the early eighteenth century a considerable number of Congregational churches had been established in northern New Jersey which looked to the graduates of Harvard and Yale for their ministers.[1] Thus it came about that Jonathan Dickinson, a native of Massachusetts—born in Hatfield in 1688—and prepared for the ministry at Yale, came to Elizabethtown, New Jersey, to have charge of the Congregational church there in 1708.

I

After the formation of the first Presbyteries and the Synod of Philadelphia in 1716, the Congregational churches in New Jersey and on Long Island were invited to become members of these Presbyterian bodies, and eventually practically all of them did so. In 1717 Jonathan Dickinson joined the Philadelphia Presbytery and was soon the acknowledged leader of American Presbyterian-

---

[1] Thomas Jefferson Wertenbaker, *The Founding of American Civilization: The Middle Colonies* (New York, 1938), chapter iv, "The Puritan in New Jersey."

ism. For forty years he continued in the ministry of Elizabethtown and it was in his study that the College of New Jersey began its long and distinguished life, and he was its first president. He was noted for "uncommon sagasity, calm judgment and unshrinking firmness, tempered, however, with the spirit of Christian forebearance and moderation. . . ." In the great controversy that arose in Presbyterianism—in Scotland, North Ireland, England, and America—over the question of compelling all candidates for the ministry to subscribe to the Westminster Confession of Faith, Jonathan Dickinson took the lead in guiding the American Presbyterians into a wise and moderate course. He was the author of the Adopting Act of 1729. Though a strict Calvinist himself, Dickinson opposed creeds and confessions of faith "drawn up by uninspired men." He held that strict subscription to a creed, instead of being a bond of union, would be a major cause of disunion. He cites the examples of the early church, in which disunity arose "from the corrupt fountain of impositions and subscriptions." Subscriptions to a creed, he held, "are not necessary to the being or well-being of a church unless hatred, variance, emulation, wrath, strife, sedition and heresies are necessary to that end." Accordingly the Adopting Act of 1729 contained within it a provision that if any minister or candidate "shall have any scruple . . . with respect to any article or articles" of the Confession or Catechism he shall so state at the time of making his declaration, and if the Synod or Presbytery decided that the article or articles about which he entertains scruples are "not essential and necessary in doctrine, worship or government" he shall be admitted. In other words, subscription was required only to necessary and essential articles, and since the Act did not state which were necessary and essential, it meant that there was a large degree of latitude, determined by the theological complexion of the Presbytery before whom the candidate appeared. Without the wise and moderate leadership furnished by Jonathan Dickinson, American colonial Presbyterianism might well have divided and redivided into many contending bodies, which would have been fatal to its usefulness.[1]

When the great revival began in New Jersey, Jonathan Dickinson did not at once join with the revivalists, for he was too level-headed to be swept along by such extreme leadership as that furnished by Gilbert Tennent. One of the determining factors which drew such men as Dickinson and Burr to the revivalist side was the expulsion of the revivalistic New Brunswick Presbytery from the Synod of Philadelphia. Dickinson held that the New Brunswick Presbytery and their adherents had as full a right to sit in the Synod as any others and their expulsion was a violation of the broad spirit of tolerance.

Once identified with the revivalists, however, Dickinson took a leading part, furnishing wise leadership in the revivalistic New York Synod as he had in the older Philadelphia Synod. In November 1739, he had sent an invitation to Whitefield to preach in his meetinghouse as he

---

[1] William W. Sweet, *Religion in Colonial America* (New York, 1942), 263-267.

journeyed westward from New York, and again in April 1740, Whitefield preached in Dickinson's church. Thus Dickinson put himself on record as a supporter of revivals, though, as was to be expected, his was a moderating influence upon the extreme fanaticism and extravagance which characterized the revival in numerous places. One of the most telling defenses of the revival was written by Dickinson in the form of a dialogue between a minister and a gentleman of his congregation regarding the revival going on in America.[2] First printed anonymously in Boston in 1742, and reprinted under Dickinson's name in Philadelphia in 1743, it was widely circulated.

As was to be expected there was no name calling or rabid denunciations in Dickinson's revivalistic preaching, though he wrote and preached with vigor. An example of his preaching is the sermon on *Conversion* first published in a little volume of *Discourses* in Boston in 1743.[3]

The text of this sermon is Ephesians 2:4–5. "But God,

---

[2] The full title of this pamphlet is: *A Display of God's Special Grace, in a Familiar Dialogue, between a Minister and a Gentleman of his Congregation about the Work of God in the Conviction and Conversion of Sinners, so Remarkably of late begun and going on in these American parts: Wherein the objections against some uncommon appearance among us are distinctly considered, mistakes rectified, and the work itself particularly proved to be from the Holy Spirit; With an Addition in a Second Conference, relating to sundry Antinomian principles, beginning to obtain in some places.* To which is prefixed an Attestation of several ministers of Boston (Boston, 1742). Published anonymously. Reprinted with the title, *A Display of God's Special Grace* by the Reverend Mr. Jonathan Dickinson, Minister of the Gospel at Elizabethtown in New Jersey (Philadelphia, 1743).

[3] Jonathan Dickinson, *The True Scriptural Doctrine Concerning Some Important Points of Christian Faith* (Boston, 1742). (Reprinted, Philadelphia, 1876.)

who is rich in mercy, for his great love wherewith he loved us, Even when we were dead in sins, hath quickened us together with Christ, (by grace ye are saved.)"

As was generally true of all eighteenth-century preachers, Dickinson developed his theme most minutely, under many heads and subheads. After an introduction explaining the implications of the text, the theme is treated under two main heads: first, "in what manner the Spirit of God quickens dead sinners, and brings them into a state of spiritual life." Second, "in what respect this quickening and sanctifying change is to be attributed to the rich mercy and grace of God." Under the heading *Improvement* he stresses two points: First, "the dreadful danger of placing any confidence or dependence upon any attainments of our own, for salvation." Second, "this gives direction and encouragement to poor distressed sinners to repair to the fountain of spiritual grace, to have God fulfill in them all the good pleasure of his. goodness, and the work of faith with power." Then follows a direct appeal to his hearers:

Do you want converting and sanctifying grace? Here is a full supply. From Christ's fullness you may all receive; and even grace for grace.

. . . .

Do you want strengthening grace? Here you may repair for that also. "His grace is sufficient for you, and his strength is made perfect in weakness."

. . . . . .

Do you want persevering grace? You may be "kept by his power through faith unto salvation." And in dependence upon him, you may have a supporting confidence, that "neither death, nor life, nor angels, nor principalities, nor powers, nor things present, nor things to come, nor height, nor depth, nor any other creature, shall be able to separate you from the love of God, which is in Jesus Christ our Lord."

Are you humbly sensible, that you have no qualifications to recommend you to the favour of God? Come to this fountain of grace, in your lost and abject condition, as you are. Come poor, wretched, miserable, blind and naked, though you have nothing but guilt and pollution to bring with you; here is mercy, rich mercy freely offered.

There is no hell and brimstone in Dickinson's preaching. In stressing the "dreadful danger of placing any confidence or dependence upon any attainments of our own for salvation," he says:

.   .   .   .   .   .

If I have any knowledge of the gospel of Christ, or any acquaintance with his method of divine grace in the conversion of sinners, they who raise their expectations of happiness from any other grounds than the sovereignty of God's free grace, as has been described above, will find in the conclusion that they have compassed themselves about with sparks of their own kindling; and what they must receive at the hands of God will be to lie down in sorrow.

.   .   .   .   .   .

How terrible will their amazement prove when they find their false confidences are rejected, and have undone them to all eternity! To have our hopes vanish and our expectations cut off, in things temporal, though many times accompanied with circumstances dismal enough, is but light and trivial, compared to an eternal disappointment. Who can imagine the dreadfulness of being miserable for EVER and EVER! Can the awful thought be entertained without horror and astonishment.

Such preaching did not arouse antagonisms, though it can easily be understood how it caused much heart-searching on the part of the hearers.

Besides the work of the ministry Jonathan Dickinson was also a practicing physician, and was accounted one of the best of his day. He was interested in healing bodies, but his chief interest was to help men sick in spirit to come to the great Physician.

II

Jonathan Edwards' commanding part in the great colonial revivals is so well known and he has, in recent years, received so much scholarly consideration, that it will not be necessary to do more than to call attention to some of the principal books that deal with his life and work. Jonathan Edwards, the philosopher and theologian, has received far more attention than has Jonathan Edwards, the preacher and revivalist. There has recently, however, appeared a life of Edwards by Ola Elizabeth Winslow [1] which deals primarily with his life as distinct from his thought. She has omitted, as she states, any full discussion

---

[1] Ola Elizabeth Winslow, *Jonathan Edwards* (New York, 1940).

of the "sweep and complexity of his ideas, their roots, their relation to the thought of his own day and their impact on the thought of the men who came after him." This she has done purposely with full awareness of the great importance of Jonathan Edwards as a philosopher. The result is a fascinating study of one whose whole life was centered in religion. "Religion was his starting point and his goal. It was his element. In it he breathed and thought and came to life as a leader of men." [2]

Another recent biography is that by Arthur Cushman McGiffert, Jr.,[3] which deals primarily with Edwards as a thinker, though it presents also an excellent appraisal of Edwards' part in the revival and as a preacher, especially in the chapter "Religion Come Alive."

From 1727 to 1750 Jonathan Edwards was the minister of the Northampton Church, a twenty-three-year pastorate. In these years he was primarily a preacher and, until the example of Whitefield jarred him out of his old ways, he was a manuscript preacher. He was never a revivalist in the usually accepted sense. Nor, contrary to the generally accepted notion, did he preach primarily upon terrifying themes such as the wrath of God and the endless punishment of sinners. As Miss Winslow has shown,[4] usually he

---

[2] *Ibid.*, 2.

[3] *Jonathan Edwards* (New York, 1932). Other books on Edwards are A. V. G. Allen, *Jonathan Edwards* (Boston, 1890), for many years the best study of Edwards' theology. H. B. Parkes, *Jonathan Edwards, the Fiery Puritan* (New York, 1930), weak in theology and the title a complete misnomer. Clarence H. Faust and Thomas H. Johnson, *Jonathan Edwards* (New York, Cincinnati, Chicago, 1935); selections from Edwards' writings with Introduction and notes.

[4] *Op. cit.*, 137.

was a "quiet-spoken teacher, and a kindly though unsparing critic of men's conduct in the light of their religious obligations." The fact is, however, that he did preach a number of hell-fire and brimstone sermons, and with terrifying effect upon his hearers. To us of this day those sermons seem incredible. Here are some paragraphs from his sermon on "The Justice of God in the Damnation of Sinners," a sermon based on the premise of the absolute sovereignty of God.[5]

It is meet that God should order all these things according to His own pleasure. By reason of his greatness and glory by which he is infinitely above all, He is worthy to be sovereign and that His pleasure should in all things take place; He is worthy that He should make Himself His end, and that He should make nothing but His own wisdom His rule in pursuing that end, without asking leave or counsel of any, and without giving any account of any of His matters. . . .

You are in God's hands, and it is uncertain what He will do with you. It may be your portion to "suffer eternal burnings; and your fears are not without grounds; you have reason to fear and tremble every moment." But whatever God does with you . . . God's justice is glorious in it.

Then follows a list of the sins of which those who are sitting in the pews have been guilty; in which they have shown their contempt of the great sovereign God. He then asks:

Seeing you thus disregard so great a God, is it a heinous thing for God to slight you, a little, wretched, despicable,

---

[5] *The Works of President Edwards*, 8 vols. (Worcester, 1809), II. Sermon VIII, 326–374, 396–421.

creature; a worm, a mere nothing, and less than nothing; a vile insect that has risen up in contempt against the majesty of heaven and earth?

Then toward the end of the sermon:

Thus I have proposed some things to your consideration, which if you are not exceedingly blind, senseless, and perverse, will stop your mouth, and convince you that you stand justly condemned before God, and that He would in no wise deal hardly with you, but altogether justly, in denying you any mercy, and in refusing to hear your prayers, let you pray never so earnestly, and never so often, and continue it never so long; and that God may utterly disregard your tears and moans, your heavy heart, your earnest desires, your great endeavors; and that he may cast you into eternal destruction, without any regard to your welfare, denying you converting grace, and giving you over to Satan, and at last cast you into the lake that burns with fire and brimstone, to be there to eternity, having no rest day or night, forever glorifying his justice upon you, in the presence of the holy angels and the presence of the Lamb.

In the sermon on "The Eternity of Hell's Torments" from the text "These shall go away into everlasting punishment" [6] (Matt. 25:46) he sets forth at the beginning what he intends to prove:

. . . I shall show that it is not inconsistent with the justice of God to inflict an eternal punishment. To evince this, I shall use only one argument, viz., that sin is heinous enough to deserve such punishment and such a punishment is no more

---

[6] *Ibid.*, Sermon X, 396–421.

than proportionable to the evil or demerit of sin. If the evil of sin be infinite, as the punishment is, then it is manifest that the punishment is no more than proportionate to the sin punished, and is no more than sin deserves. . . .

There is no evading the force of this reasoning but by denying that God, the sovereign of the universe, is infinitely glorious; which I presume none of my hearers will adventure to do.

Here is a ruthless logical syllogism applied to God in His relation to sinful men, and we of this day know that it does not apply. John Wesley was accustomed to say: "You cannot reason concerning spiritual things."

In his most famous sermon, "Sinners in the Hands of an Angry God" by which his preaching has been most unjustly judged, occurs this fear-inspiring sentence:

And though he will know that you cannot bear the weight of omnipotence treading upon you, yet he will not regard that, but he will crush you under his feet without mercy; he will crush out your blood, and make it fly, and it shall be sprinkled on his garments, so as to stain all his raiment. He will not only hate you, but he will have you in the utmost contempt; no place shall be fit for you, but under his feet to be trodden down as the mire of the streets.

Is it any wonder that some began to say that Jonathan Edwards was confusing God with the Devil?

Not only did Jonathan Edwards preach on the terrors of God's law, for the purpose of arousing fear on the part of sinners, but he staunchly defended it. He says:

If there be really a hell of such dreadful and never-ending torments, as is generally supposed, of which multitudes are in great danger—and into which the greater part of them in Christian countries do actually from generation to generation fall, for want of a sense of its terribleness . . . ? Why should they not be told as much of the truth as can be? If I am in danger of going to hell, I should be glad to know as much as I possibly can of the dreadfulness of it. If I am very prone to neglect due care to avoid it, he does me the best kindness, who does most to represent to me the truth in the case, that sets forth my misery and danger in the liveliest manner.

.   .   .   .

. . . If any of you who are heads of families saw one of your children in a house all on fire, and in imminent danger of being consumed in the flames, yet seemed to be very insensible of its danger, and neglected to escape after you had called to it—would you go on to speak to it only in a cold indifferent manner? Would you not cry aloud, and call earnestly to it, and represent the danger it was in, and its own folly in delaying, in the most lively manner of which you were capable? [7]

Preachers who preach of hell, and warn people to avoid it in a mild manner, he says, "contradict themselves." Some people think it is an unreasonable thing "to fright persons to heaven; but I think it is a reasonable thing to fright persons away from hell."

There are more than five hundred of Edwards' sermons

---

[7] *The Distinguishing Marks of a Work of the Spirit of God*, in the *Works of President Edwards*, 4 vols. (New York and Boston, 1843), I, 535–538.

in print and in manuscript, and it is only fair to state again that sermons such as those from which these quotations are taken constitute only a very small proportion of his total sermon output. To judge his preaching justly we must bear in mind those tender passages in his greatest theological work, *A Treatise Concerning Religious Affections,* and that under Whitefield's preaching at Northampton, which dwelt largely with God's infinite love and pity for men, Jonathan Edwards sat weeping behind him in the pulpit. Edwards, in spite of all his logic, believed profoundly that the "sense of God" is an emotional experience, not an intellectual one. And this is where Jonathan Edwards and John Wesley come together.

We catch a glimpse of a very different Jonathan Edwards in a sermon that he preached in 1741 at the burial of Rev. William Williams, a minister at Hatfield. The text is the story of the burial of John the Baptist. His first point is that Christ is one that is ready to pity the afflicted.

The heart that is full of grief wants vent, and desires to pour out its complaint; but it seeks a compassionate friend to pour it out before.

Christ is such a one, above all others. . . .

Miss Winslow has well stated that the *central fact* in the great upheaval in American life, which we call the Great Awakening, and with which Jonathan Edwards had so much to do, was that religion is a personal matter; that it is an "inner experience or it is nothing." In his *Treatise Concerning Religious Affections* and through his own example in his preaching, as well as in his pastoral ministrations, Jonathan Edwards made religious emotion theologically and intellectually respectable. This fact is basic [8] to any adequate understanding of the course of revivalism in America.

---

[8] Winslow, *op. cit.*, 212–214.

CHAPTER FIVE

THE REVIVALISTS WHO BROUGHT RELIGION TO THE COMMON MAN

I

IT MAY SEEM somewhat strange that this chapter on re-vivalism and the common man should begin with an account of the activities of an Anglican clergyman, Devereux Jarratt.

Devereux Jarratt, rector of Bath Parish, in Dinwiddie County, Virginia, was one of the few revivalistic clergy-men among the colonial Anglicans. Charles Pettigrew, the leading Anglican clergyman in colonial North Carolina in the latter seventeen hundreds, and Uzal Ogden, the Anglican minister in Newton, New Jersey, at the same time, leaned to some degree towards revivalism; and both gave aid and advice to the early Methodist itinerants in their respective vicinities. Jarratt's revivalistic activities, however, were far more significant.

A native of Virginia (born 1733) and largely self-edu-cated, Devereux Jarratt, while tutoring in a Presbyterian family in central Virginia, came under evangelical influ-ence and finally entered into a definite conversion experi-ence which he has fully described in his *Autobiography*, as follows:

Such a bright manifestation of the redeemer's all-sufficiency and willingness to save, and such a divine confidence to rely on him, I never had till that moment—it was a little heaven upon earth—so ravishing, so delightful.

On his conversion he at once determined to enter the ministry and was inclined towards the Presbyterians, and was prejudiced against the Anglican Church, because of the loose lives of so many of its clergymen, but he says:

I began to doubt a good deal respecting the decrees of Predestination and Election. These tenets did not appear so reconcileable to the divine attributes as I might once think.[1]

This, and perhaps also his Anglican background, finally led him to enter the Anglican Church. After some special preparation and study, he sailed for England in 1762 to secure ordination. While in England he heard both John Wesley and Whitefield preach, though he states that he got little edification from either. Returning to Virginia he secured a parish in Dinwiddie County and here he remained until the end of his life in 1801.

He thus describes the religious situation in his parish when he arrived:

I found the principles of the gospel—the nature and condition of man—the plan of salvation through Christ—and *the nature and necessity of spiritual regeneration* as little known and thought of as if the people had never a church or heard a sermon in their lives.[2]

---

[1] *The Life of the Reverend Devereux Jarratt, Rector of Bath Parish in Dinwiddie County, Virginia* (Baltimore, 1806), 49, 58, 87–88, 89. Written by himself. In a series of letters addressed to the Rev. John Coleman, one of the ministers of the Protestant Episcopal Church in Maryland.
[2] *Ibid.*, 83, 85.

I encountered a gross ignorance of divine things, combined with conceited wisdom and moral rectitude.

The members of his congregations said: "We have never heard any thing till now, of conversion, and the new birth."

Jarratt set about at once to try to remedy the low state of vital religion in the three congregations making up his parish, by preaching the "self-abasing doctrine of free grace . . . in a close, plain, searching, pungent manner." At first the people were greatly offended, but it was not long until conditions began to change. Soon a widespread religious concern began to be manifest and his churches were crowded with hearers. But he did not confine his efforts to the churches, but held meetings in private houses and visited people wherever he could find them. The middle classes were the first to respond, and then the poorer people, who had never had any direct contact with the church or clergymen, began to be interested.

Jarratt gives the following general plan of his preaching. His first concern was to make sinners feel their situation and be sensible of their guilt, danger, and helplessness. To bring about this result he bore down upon the doctrine of original sin. "Instead of moral harangues, and advising my hearers in a cool, dispassionate manner, to walk the prim- rose paths of a decided, sublime, and elevated virtue, and not to tread in the foul tracts of disgraceful vice" he states that:

I endeavored to expose, in the most alarming colors, the guilt of sin, the entire depravity of human nature, the awful danger mankind are in, by nature and practice, the tremendous curse under which all men find themselves and their utter inability to evade the sentence of the law and the stroke of divine justice by their own power, merit or good works.

His next endeavor was to press home the conviction that the only hope was in Jesus Christ and to bring them to "rest on him" for complete salvation. And then, finally, he exhorted those who believed, to be careful to maintain good works, and go on to perfection.

This type of preaching gained for Jarratt an unenviable reputation among the general run of the Anglican clergy in Virginia. He says:

I stood alone, not knowing of one clergyman in Virginia likeminded with myself; yea, I was opposed, and reproached by the clergy, called an enthusiast, fanatic, visionary, dissenter, Presbyterian, madman, and whatnot; yet was I so well convinced of the utility and importance of the truths I declared and the doctrines I preached, that no clamor, opposition, or reproach could daunt my spirit or move me from my purpose and manner of preaching or induce me to give flattering titles to any man. I durst not prophesy smooth things, nor flatter the highest in their follies and vanities.

In 1793 Jarratt published a volume of sermons entitled *Sermons on Various and Important Subjects in Practical Divinity.*[3] He states in his preface that he had always

---

[3] Devereux Jarratt, *Sermons on Various and Important Subjects, in Practical Divinity Adapted to the Plainest Capacities and Suited to the Family and Closet* (Raleigh, 1793).

preached *extempore* so that the sermons are not just as they were preached, though they are on the same texts and contain the substance of the original sermons. The subjects are suggestive of the revivalistic nature of his preaching. Compared to the sermons of Edwards and Davies they are very brief—clearly outlined—and always ending with a personal application. Some typical subjects are "The Righteous and the Wicked Characterized; and Their Different Reward Pointed Out"; "The Necessity and Advantage of Seeking the Lord"; "God's Call to Sinners; or a Preparation for Death and Judgment." In a sermon entitled "The Pious Minister's Complaint over the Unsteadiness and Incorrigibleness of his Flock" his text is "O Ephraim, what shall I do unto thee? O Judah, what shall I do unto thee? For your goodness is as a morning cloud, and as the early dew it goeth away," a particularly effective text on which to base an appeal for steadfastness. In his application he is very personal:

It is ten thousand pities that so much love and goodness should be abused; and your precious souls be eternally ruined, and burn in hell forever; after all that Jesus Christ hath done to bless and to save you. Permit me to be more pointed, and address you as it were by name. O drunkard, what shall I do unto thee? How shall I persuade you to forsake this sottish practice which degrades the rational nature, makes the man a beast, and exposes him to the jest and ridicule, even of his own children and servants, wastes his time and fortune, disqualifies him for business, and destroys his soul forever. Remember those intoxicating cups, you now indulge, will put into your hand the cup of divine indignation, the bitter dregs of which you will drink to endless ages.[4]

Then follow in similar vein the answers to the questions: "O swearer, what shall I do unto thee?" . . . "O Sabbath-breaker, what shall I do unto thee?" . . . "O sons and daughters of pride and vanity, what shall I do unto thee?" . . . "O Liar, what shall I do unto thee?"

As has already been noted, Jarratt's significance as a revivalistic leader was greatly enlarged by his willingness to co-operate with the Methodist itinerants when they appeared on the American scene after 1770. From that time until the end of the Revolution, when they withdrew from the Anglicans to form an independent communion, his work was merged with theirs.

II

We have come now to a consideration of those colonial revivalists whose work and influence was most widespread among the common people, and who laid the foundation for the great popular churches. I refer to the Baptist farmer-preachers and the early Methodist circuit-riders. Uneducated, as far as the schools were concerned, they left behind scant records of their lives and few written sermons. Theirs were "the short and simple annals of the poor."

The two best sources of information concerning the preachers who carried forward the Baptist phase of the

---

[4] *Ibid.,* 193.

Virginia and North Carolina revivals are Robert B. Semple's *History of the . . . Baptists in Virginia*[1] and James B. Taylor's *Lives of Virginia Baptist Ministers*.

The man who occupied before his conversion the highest social position among the Virginia Baptist preachers was Samuel Harris. Born in Hanover County in 1724, by his middle thirties he had become a man of substance. Not only had he acquired considerable property but held numerous offices, as church warden, sheriff, burgess of the county, and colonel of militia. On one of his military missions he stopped, more or less by chance, at a place where some Baptists were gathering for a meeting. His conscience was stirred by what he heard, and soon afterwards he openly professed conversion. In 1759, the year succeeding his conversion, he began to preach in Pittsylvania County where he resided, and in neighboring counties. This he continued for some ten years. Thereafter Harris became a constant traveler and ranged throughout Virginia and North Carolina on endless preaching excursions. He preached wherever people could be found to listen. Soon after his conversion he was led to preach to the soldiers at the Fort with which he had formerly been connected. In the course of his sermon he was interrupted by some of his officer acquaintances who accused him of being drunk or mad; to which Harris responded in the words of Paul, "I am not mad, most noble gentlemen."

[1] Robert B. Semple, *A History of the Rise and Progress of the Baptists in Virginia* (Richmond, 1810). James B. Taylor, *Lives of Virginia Baptist Ministers* (Richmond, 1838). See also W. M. Gewehr, *The Great Awakening in Virginia, op. cit.*, chapter v, "The Baptist Revival."

Like other early Baptist preachers in Virginia, Harris suffered considerable persecution though no doubt his social position saved him from the extreme opposition experienced by some of the other Baptist preachers. In his manner he was gentle and his preaching was largely an appeal to the heart. His better education undoubtedly gave him a larger hearing among the upper classes, but his main work, as was that of the other Baptist preachers of the time, was to the common people who had been largely overlooked and neglected. Samuel Harris was representative of a new type of religious leadership arising in America. Such leadership could not function in the New England meetinghouse nor even in the backwoods Presbyterian churches, such as those in which Samuel Davies ministered, but it could and did function effectively on the frontier.

Another, among the many Virginia Baptist revivalists, was James Ireland. A native of Scotland, he had been brought up under Presbyterian influences. On his arrival in America he taught school in a godless community in northern Virginia, where only a small handful of Quakers maintained worship in a private house. He describes himself as "not only willing to be wicked, but studied to be so." He had a certain gift at writing verse and was requested by a pious young man to compose a poem on a religious subject. This proved to be the means of his conversion, though after an inner struggle—so characteristic of conversion experiences of the time. He at once became interested in helping others in securing a similar experience, and soon there was a little nucleus of religiously-minded people in the community where he lived. There was no regular preaching, however, until Elder John Picket, a Baptist itinerant, happened to hear of the religious stirrings in that community and traveled sixty miles to visit the neighborhood. Soon after this Ireland began to address religious meetings, though without authorization from any church. In fact, he was not as yet a church member, and it was some time before he was willing to accept the rite of baptism according to Baptist practice, because of his Presbyterian training.

From this time forward James Ireland [2] gave himself completely to the work of the ministry, and for many years was the pastor of three congregations west of the Blue Ridge. Better educated than most of the Baptist preachers of his time, he soon became in the words of Semple "eminent as a preacher." His style "was handsome, though plain . . . his manner . . . affectionate and tender." He was often deeply affected himself while preaching. He is described as an eloquent man, though his eloquence was not of the flashy kind, consisting of fair words and fine speeches. "His arguments were close and pertinent . . . his exhortations . . . warm and pathetic." [3]

The fact that the Baptist preachers were generally men with little education, the appeal of whose preaching was almost entirely to the emotions, naturally encouraged extravagances. But as a whole they were men of good com-

---

[2] James Ireland, *Life* (Winchester, 1819).
[3] Semple, *op. cit.*, 426.

mon sense, often superior in native ability, with profound religious convictions and a sacrificial zeal that did not flinch even before persecution. They felt themselves called of God and they did not hesitate to go wherever that call seemed to lead. Most of them were unwilling to secure a license for preaching, as required by Virginia, since that seemed to them a violation of their first great principle—complete religious liberty and complete separation of the Church from the State. As a consequence persecution fell heavily upon them. Their mode of preaching and certain peculiar mannerisms brought ridicule. One such mannerism was called the "holy whine," which consisted in the rising and falling of the voice, supposedly to relieve the strain of outdoor preaching. They also were inclined to indulge in exaggerated gesticulations and "odd whoops" and their impassioned manner often "moved their congregations to . . . tremblings, screams and fallings." [4]

The Baptists naturally found their largest following among the poor, illiterate, and ignorant people and they gained the contempt of the upper-class Anglicans and Presbyterians. But religion has a strange way of lifting people out of the lowest social stratum in a relatively short time, and that is what happened to the Baptists in Virginia and the Carolinas.

III

The Methodist colonial revivalists were of three kinds; first the local preacher immigrants who came to the colo-

---

[4] Gewehr, *op cit.*, 114.

nies on their own volition, and once here, they, of their own accord, began to spread the Methodist gospel. A second group were the lay preacher missionaries, sent over by John Wesley and the English Methodist Conference; a third group was made up of the native American preachers, who by the end of the Revolution had become the dominant element in American Methodism. Examples of the first group are Philip Embury, who started the first Methodist Class in New York in 1766; and Robert Strawbridge, who is the father of American Methodism in Maryland and Virginia. Belonging to this group also are Robert Williams, the first Methodist preacher to come into contact with Devereux Jarratt; and Captain Thomas Webb, a convert of Wesley himself. Webb came to America on a military mission, but was able to combine a great deal of Methodist pioneering in connection with his official duties. The second group, the official missionaries, were eight in number, and, of the eight, Joseph Pilmoor, Richard Boardman, Francis Asbury, Thomas Rankin, and George Shadford are the most important. Of the native American group William Watters, Philip Gatch, Freeborn Garrettson and Benjamin Abbott stand out the most prominently.[1]

All of these groups were constituted of men without formal training for the ministry, and they were all zealous

---

[1] For a characterization of each of these groups and an estimate of their contributions, see W. W. Sweet, *Men of Zeal: the Romance of American Methodist Beginnings* (New York, 1935), especially chapters ii, "Irish Local Preacher Immigrants and American Methodist Origins"; iii, "Wesley's Missionaries to America," and iv, "The American Revolution and the Rise of the Native Preachers."

for the spread of the Gospel of Christ under the Methodist banner. We will let the activities of Robert Strawbridge typify the local preacher immigrants.

Robert Strawbridge was a native of County Leitrim, Ireland, where he had already become a Methodist and a lay preacher. He came to America with his young wife somewhere between 1760 and 1766 and settled on a farm near Sams Creek in Frederick County, Maryland, where a monument now stands to commemorate his part in the bringing of Methodism to America. Perhaps it was the lure of cheap and fertile land which proved the determining factor in his coming, just as it was of the great majority of his countrymen. Hardly was he settled in his new home than we find him preaching to his neighbors. They were soon formed into a Methodist class and a rude log meetinghouse erected about a mile from his house. From this beginning Strawbridge became a tireless itinerant, journeying to and fro over a large area. We find traces of him in both eastern and western Maryland, in Delaware, Virginia, and Pennsylvania. He was particularly effective in stirring the interest of younger men and inducing them to become preachers, and to him belongs the credit of raising up the first native American preachers.

His was an independent spirit, finding difficulty in fitting into the more or less rigid pattern of Methodist organization which John Wesley's official representatives brought to America. It is significant that his name appears among the regular Methodist appointments but one year, an indication of his free-lance character. He was energetic, fiery and fluent in his preaching, and devoted to the spread of the Gospel of Christ as he understood it. He was more interested in people than in organization, a fact that made him a thorn in the flesh to the disciplinarians, Thomas Rankin and Francis Asbury.

Thomas Webb was a captain in the British army; he was sent to America, probably in 1766, as barrack officer at Albany, where a contingent of British troops were quartered, as a part of the new colonial policy instituted by Lord Grenville. One of Wesley's own converts, he licensed him to preach. Unlike many others, when he came to America, Captain Webb brought all of his religion with him and at every opportunity exercised his gifts. He was the chief support in the erection of Wesley Chapel in New York, having subscribed the largest sum for the building; he was the first to bring the Methodist gospel to Philadelphia, and aided in the purchase of St. George's Church there, the oldest Methodist church in continuous use now in America. As a preacher he won the respect of educated men. Wesley writes in his *Journal* after hearing Captain Webb preach:

I admire the wisdom of God in still raising up various preachers according to the various tastes of men. The Captain is all life and fire; therefore, although he is not deep or regular, yet many who would not hear a better preacher, flock to hear him. . . .[2]

---

[2] *The Journal of the Reverend John Wesley* (Nehemiah Curnock, Ed.), 8 vols. (London, 1909–1916), V, 497.

John Adams while in attendance upon the Continental Congress in Philadelphia was accustomed to visit the churches of the several denominations in the city, and has recorded his opinions of the sermons he heard in his diary or in letters to his wife. One evening in 1774 he heard Captain Webb and has thus recorded his opinion of the sermon:

In the evening I went to the Methodist meeting and heard Mr. Webb, the old soldier, who first came to America in the character of a quartermaster under General Braddock. He is one of the most fluent, eloquent men I ever heard; he reaches the imagination and touches the passions very well, and expresses himself with great propriety. (May 28, 1774) [3]

Asbury called him "an Israelite indeed" and records the fact in his *Journal* that he heard "Captain W. preached a good sermon in the evening."

Of Wesley's official representatives in America George Shadford was, perhaps, the most effective revivalistic preacher. He came to America in 1773 with Thomas Rankin, returning to England five years later. In his young manhood he had been a soldier in the British army, and on his discharge had come into contact with the Methodists and "entered upon a religious life." He had been a member of the Conference but five years when he volunteered as a missionary to America. He began his American preaching in Philadelphia, but his principal work as a revivalist

---

[3] *The Works of John Adams* (Charles Francis Adams, Ed.), 10 vols. (Boston, 1850), II, 401.

was performed in Virginia where he was in close coopera-
tion with Devereux Jarratt. It was during these years
(1775–1776) that the first real Methodist revival in America took place. The center of the revival was in Brunswick
County and culminated in the winter and spring of 1776.
It spread throughout Jarratt's parish in Dinwiddie County,
and into adjoining counties. The number of converts was
phenomenal, from ten to twenty a day, for days and weeks
together. Jarratt has left an account of this revival in a
letter to John Wesley which Asbury placed in his *Journal*.[4]

In this narrative Jarratt states that Shadford in his
preaching confirmed the doctrine he had long preached,
with the result that sinners were powerfully convinced.
"Many were panting and groaning for pardon" and en-
treated God "with strong cries and tears to save them
from the remains of inbred sin, to 'sanctify them throughout . . .'" Shadford was the chief preaching instrument
in this revival, though Jarratt was working "quietly but
zealously and effectively all the time."[5] Many societies
were formed among his parishioners and he requested that
his parish be made a part of the Brunswick circuit.

Some of the emotional excesses which occurred in this
revival were distasteful to Jarratt. These occurred when
the hearers were mostly men and women of the unlettered
classes, and frequently great numbers of Negroes were
also present. Not infrequently whole congregations "would
be bathed in tears; sometimes their cries would be so loud

---

[4] *Journal*, I, 208–220.
[5] Gewehr, *op. cit.*, 148–153.

that the preacher's voice could not be heard. Some were seized with trembling; some dropped to the floor and lay for a time as though dead. . . ." [6]

As Shadford was embarking for America he received this letter from John Wesley:

Dear George: The time has arrived for you to embark for America; you must go down to Bristol, where you will meet with Thomas Rankin, Captain Webb, and his wife. I let you loose, George, on the great continent of America; publish your message in the open face of the sun and do all the good you can. [7]

Reading between the lines of this characteristic letter of Wesley's, one can catch his fatherly affection for this young man setting out for America. Evidently he was a favorite, as he later came to be with Asbury.

As the revolt of the Colonies mounted higher and higher, Shadford became increasingly concerned as to his duty; whether he should remain in America or return to England. He tells us that it was impossible for him to take the test oath required in Maryland and Virginia as he had taken the oath of allegiance to the King twice, and now found himself unable to renounce him forever. "I dare not," he says, "play with fast and loose oaths, and swallow them in such a manner." This decided him to return to England, which he did in 1778. Now only Francis Asbury

---

[6] Quoted in Gewehr, *op. cit.*, 153.
[7] *The Letters of the Reverend John Wesley*, etc. (John Telford, Ed.), 8 vols. (London, 1931), VI, 23.

was left of the eight whom Wesley had sent to America, and of the seven who had returned, Shadford was the only one whose going was a loss to American Methodism.

Of the native American Methodist preachers Benjamin Abbott was perhaps the most unusual. He was converted under the preaching of Philip Gatch, another of the more prominent native preachers. Born in 1732, and a native of Pennsylvania, Abbott's work as an itinerant was confined to the Middle Colonies and Maryland. Immediately on his conversion he began to tell of his transformed life and was soon attracting multitudes to hear him. Though rude and ungrammatical in speech, he had a gift at coining unusual phrases and frequently great emotional excitement was occasioned as a result of his rugged eloquence. Asbury, after hearing him preach in February 1781, remarks in his *Journal*: his (Abbott's) "words came with power," people "fall to the ground under him, and sink into a passive state, helpless, stiff, motionless." A contemporary biographer states that "he was one of the wonders of America, no man's copy, an uncommon zealot." He preached sanctification continuously, "and what was best of all, he lived it."

Robert Southey in his *Life of Wesley* [8] devotes several pages to Benjamin Abbott and characterizes him as a sincere and well-meaning enthusiast on the verge of madness. In Abbott's preaching he often took advantage of immediate happenings and with overwhelming effect. Once he was asked to say something at a funeral, following the service conducted by an Anglican clergyman. As he began to

---

[8] *The Life of Wesley; and the Rise and Progress of Methodism* (New York, 1820), 2 vols., II, 206–209.

speak a fearful storm arose, and the people, many of whom had been on the outside, crowded into the house. The lightning and thunder were terrifying in their intensity, and the whole house shook and shuddered with every clap of thunder. In the midst of the storm's raging, Abbott compared the storm with the coming of Christ in all his "spleandour, with all the armies of heaven, to judge the world and to take vengence on the ungodly." It may be, he cried out, "that he will descend in the next clap of thunder!" All through the house the people screamed and fell, but Abbott continued, and as the storm gradually passed he invited the people to flee to Christ for safety. Fourteen years afterward, when Abbott again rode that circuit, he states that he found twelve living witnesses, who told him that they were converted under the influence of that sermon. Southey remarks that it had been asserted that such preaching as that of Abbott had undoubtedly caused an increase of insanity, but even so, "the good that it produces is greater than the evil."

It is a significant fact that a large proportion of the most influential early native preachers came out of an Anglican background, particularly those from Virginia and Maryland. Among them are to be found William Watters, Philip Gatch, Freeborn Garrettson and Jesse Lee.[9] They

---

[9] We are fortunate in having fairly adequate biographies of each of these four early Methodist preachers: John M'Lean, *Sketch of Rev. Philip Gatch* (Cincinnati, 1854); William Watters, *A Short Account of the Christian Experience and Ministerial Labours of William Watters* drawn up by himself (Alexandria, Va., N. D.); Nathan Bangs, *The Life of the Rev. Freeborn Garrettson: Compiled from his Printed and Manuscript Journals, and Other Authentic Documents* (New York, 1829); LeRoy M. Lee, *The Life and Times of the Rev. Jesse Lee* (Louisville, 1848).

represent a type distinctly different from Benjamin Abbott. Philip Gatch, for instance, had a fair education according to the standards of that day. After a score or more of effective years of preaching in Maryland, Virginia, New Jersey, and Delaware, where his work resulted in adding many hundreds, if not thousands, to the church, he removed to Ohio (1787) and settled in Clermont County, some twenty miles east of Cincinnati. Here he became a recognized leader, was a member of the Constitutional Convention and later a Judge of the County Court. Though no longer traveling a circuit, it was his custom to preach in his courtroom on Sundays, during the term of the court. He continued as a local preacher to the end of his life.

Freeborn Garrettson came also from Church of England parentage, was a native of Maryland, and seems to have had a fair education. His mother was an earnest Christian and gave her son Christian instruction. His conversion came as a result of the combined influence of Strawbridge and Francis Asbury, and he began to preach in 1776. It is an interesting fact that Philip Gatch, Freeborn Garrettson, and Jesse Lee all refused to bear arms during the Revolution, and all of them met persecution because of it. Garrettson has left us this account in his *Journal* of his position on slavery (1777):

In September (1777) I went to North Carolina, to travel the Roanoke circuit, and I was sweetly drawn out in the glorious work, though my exercises were very great, particularly respecting slavery. Many times did my heart ache on account

of the slaves in this part of the country, and many tears did I
shed, both in Virginia and Carolina, while exhibiting a cruci-
fied Jesus to their view; and I bless God that my labours were
not in vain among them. I endeavored frequently to inculcate
the doctrine of freedom in a private way, and this procured me
the ill will of some, who were in the unmerciful practice. I
would often set apart times to preach to the blacks, and adapt
my discourse to them alone. . . . While many of their sable
faces were bedewed with tears, their withered hands of faith
were stretched out, and their precious souls made white in the
blood of the lamb.[10]

It was Freeborn Garrettson who was sent out to summon
the preachers to the Christmas Conference in 1784 and
from that time to the end of his life his leadership became
increasingly recognized. In 1793 he married Catharine
Livingston, daughter of the distinguished Robert R. Livingston, one of the largest land-holders in the nation.
Henceforth his home was at Rhinebeck on the Hudson, but
he did not permit that to interfere with his work as a
Methodist minister and continued active until his death,
in 1827.

The following is an account of an incident recorded by
Garrettson in his *Journal*, which took place on the Frederick circuit in Virginia in 1779:

"I visited," he says, "Shepherd's town, lying high on the
Potomac River. On the Lord's day I attended the church
[Anglican] and heard the minister preach on 'Keep Holy
the Sabbath Day'."

10 Bangs, *op. cit.*, 58–59.

This discourse, he says, took up fifteen minutes, and there was not a word spoken about "the fall of man, faith or repentance." When he had finished, Garrettson asked the liberty to speak; permission was given and he went up into the pulpit and announced as his text, "How shall we escape if we neglect so great salvation?" After his discourse one of the hearers asked the minister what he thought of the doctrine preached by the young stranger. To this the minister replied, "He seems to bring Scripture to prove it; it may be so, but if it is, I know nothing of it." [11]

IV

George Whitefield spent more than ten years of his ministry in the colonies, and his preaching tours covered the inhabited parts of America. Through the enterprise of Benjamin Franklin and other colonial printers his printed sermons were spread from New Hampshire on the north to Georgia on the south. He touched every phase of the colonial awakenings, and his preaching was effective among all classes. In London there were erected two large buildings for his use, one a large barnlike structure on the edge of the poverty-stricken section; the other a more dignified chapel near London's fashionable West End. To the tabernacle came the lowly and the poor; to the chapel came the rich and fashionable. But the preacher never trimmed his message to suit the ears of the rich.

Whitefield's adoption of Calvinistic principles, soon after his first preaching tour in the colonies, was a handicap to his work in England for it led to a break with the Wesleys,

[11] *Ibid.*, 49–50.

whose gospel appeal centered about the doctrine of free grace. It was, however, an aid to his American ministry, for there, as has been noticed, all the evangelists were preaching a personalized Calvinism. In England his converts eventually became a separate denomination, known as Calvinistic Methodists; in the colonies Whitefield tied up to no single denominational body, but served them all without favoritism, Congregationalists, Presbyterians, Baptists, Dutch Reformed, and Quakers and many others with whom he could co-operate in the work of saving souls. Though a priest in the Church of England, and appointed to succeed Wesley as rector at Savannah, Georgia—the only parish either Wesley or Whitefield ever had—his work was almost completely among people outside the Anglican communion.

For an estimate of Whitefield as a preacher we are dependent upon the testimony of those who heard him, and not upon his sermons that have appeared in print. He was not a theologian; "he was not a sermonizer in the technical sense; but he *was* a preacher, and he knew it." He had a strong and musical voice that could be heard by thousands. One time when Whitefield was in Philadelphia preaching out-of-doors, Franklin estimated that he could be heard by twenty-five thousand people. Whitefield believed in using his voice. "I love those who thunder out the word," he once said, "the Christian world is in a dead sleep. Nothing but a loud voice can awaken them out of it." [1] He was not

---

[1] Edward S. Ninde, *George Whitefield, Prophet and Preacher* (New York, 1924), especially chapter x, "Whitefield the Preacher." C. H. Maxson, *op. cit.*, chapter viii, "Whitefield the Pacificator." See also James P. Gladstone, *George Whitefield M.A., Field Preacher* (New York, 1901).

only loud and clear, but his enunciation was faultless. David Garrick, the great contemporary actor, once re-marked that if Whitefield were on the stage he could make an audience weep or tremble by his very utterance of the word "Mesopotamia." Benjamin Franklin, who often heard him preach, stated that "every accent, every emphasis, every modulation of voice was so perfectly tuned and well placed, that without being interested in the subject, one could not help being pleased with the discourse."[2]

No one seems to know when and how Whitefield pre-pared his sermons. He had no particular time for preparing. He did, however, generally arrange to have an hour alone before he preached on Sunday mornings. He seldom got through a sermon without weeping, which he justified by saying, "You blame me for weeping, but how can I help it when you will not weep for yourselves, though your souls are upon the verge of destruction and for aught I know, you are hearing your last sermon!"

He generally wore a gown when preaching and not in-frequently read prayers from the Prayer Book, though he was mighty in *extempore* prayer. He never permitted any form to hamper him; he was equally at home in the pulpit, standing on a chair in a house, or the steps of an inn, or on an elevation in a field. He was not a manuscript preacher; indeed, it is doubtful whether he ever had a scrap of paper to guide his thought while preaching. In

---

[2] See the various references to George Whitefield in *The Autobiography of Benjamin Franklin,* edited with an Introduction and notes by Oral S. Coad (New York, 1929).

his personal life he was devout and sincere and if in his earlier years he was fond of his popularity, he soon became weary of it and often said he "envied the man who could take his choice of food at an eating-house, and pass unnoticed." Whitefield published a number of prayers and they reveal the breadth of his human interest. Among them are prayers for those who desire and are seeking for the new birth; for those who feel spiritually deserted; for those under the displeasure of close friends and relatives because of their religious concern. There are prayers for laborers, for servants and Negroes, as well as for the rich. There are prayers for the sick, for travelers and sailors, and for persons in a storm at sea. His thirteen voyages across the stormy Atlantic, in those days of little sailing ships, made him particularly conscious of the terrors which storms at sea produced.

In his preaching Whitefield was a painter of pictures and often dramatic. The striking apostrophe from Jeremiah, "O earth, earth, earth, hear the words of the Lord," he often threw in in the midst of a sermon, and it never failed to electrify a crowd. An example of his dramatic appeal is his description of Peter's remorse after his denial of Christ.

Methinks I see him wringing his hands, rending his garments, stamping on the ground, and, with the self-condemned publican, smiting his breast. See how it heaves! O what piteous sighs and groans are those which come from the very bottom of his heart! Alas! it is too big to speak; but his tears, his briny, bitter, repenting tears, plainly bespeak this to be the language of his awakened soul. "Alas! where have I been? On the devil's ground. With whom have I been conversing? The devil's children. What is this that I have done? Denied the Lord of glory; with oaths and curses denied that I ever knew him. And now whither shall I go, or where shall I hide my guilty head? I have sinned against light, I have sinned against repeated tokens of his dear, distinguishing and heavenly love. I have sinned against repeated warnings, resolutions, promises, vows. I have sinned openly in the face of sun, and in the presence of my Master's enemies, and thereby have caused his name to be blasphemed. How can I think to be suffered to behold the face of, much less to be employed by, the ever-blessed Jesus any more? O Peter! thou hast undone thyself. Justly mayest thou be thrown aside like a broken vessel. God be merciful to me a sinner!"

All told Whitefield prepared sixty-three sermons for the press; twenty-six of these were written before his twenty-fifth year. As a whole they read poorly and today it is difficult to imagine how they could have produced such overwhelming effects upon the hearers. As a consequence only those who heard him could possibly know Whitefield the Preacher, for no art can print "the lightning, thunder, and rainbow."

The appeal of Whitefield's preaching is strikingly shown in the following news item which appeared in Benjamin Franklin's paper in November 1740:

On Thursday last, the Rev. Mr. Whitefield left this city, and was accompanied to Chester by about one hundred and fifty horse, and preached there to about seven thousand people. On Friday he preached twice at Willing's Town to about five thousand; on Saturday, at Newcastle, to about two thousand five hundred; and the same evening at Christina Bridge, to about three thousand; on Sunday, at White Clay Creek, he preached twice, resting about half an hour between sermons, to about eight thousand, of whom about three thousand, it is computed, came on horseback. It rained most of the time, and yet they stood in the open air.

At fifty years of age Whitefield was an old man. From the year 1736, the Sunday after his admission to deacon's orders when he preached his first sermon in Gloucester, England, until the very day of his death, September 30, 1770, his life was that of a flaming apostle, with but one consuming concern—to save souls. Although never strong in body his physical and mental energy was seemingly inexhaustible. Toward the end of his life when urged to preach less often he replied, "I had rather wear out than rust out," and he had his wish.

CHAPTER SIX

REVIVALISM AND THE WESTWARD MARCH

THE CLOSING YEARS of the eighteenth century and the opening years of the nineteenth saw an immense movement of population from the eastern seaboard into the great valleys west of the Allegheny Mountains. So great was the movement that within a generation following the adoption of the Federal Constitution eleven new states had been admitted to the Union: nothing to compare with it is recorded in the history of modern times. With the beginning of the new century the whole nation seemed veritably to be on the move. Roads swarmed with wagons laden with families and household goods. Through one Pennsylvania village on the road to Pittsburgh, toward the close of the year 1811, two hundred and thirty-six wagons and six hundred Merino sheep, passed in the course of a single day, all bound for Ohio. Even the snows of winter failed to stop the movement. Old settlers in central New York declared that they had never seen so many teams and sleighs loaded with women and children and household goods passing through to the West, as in the very midst of the winter of 1814. From Lancaster, Pennsylvania, came the report that a hundred families had passed through that town in one week; at Zanesville, Ohio, fifty wagons crossed the Muskingum in one day. Nor was this stream of population movement sporadic; it continued day after day, week after week, month after month, and year after year. Typical of the rapidity with which towns sprang up in the West is the story of Vevay, Indiana. Laid out in 1813, it was by 1816 a county seat with courthouse, schoolhouse, public library, stores, taverns, and seventy-five dwellings. It was receiving three mails a week and supported a weekly newspaper.

To bring the story of this vast American migration down to individuals, family records are revealing. Jonathan Fairbanks came to Massachusetts from England in 1633. In the town of Dedham he built a house which is still standing and has been occupied by his descendants for nine generations. Today other descendants are found living in thirty-four states of the Union. The original members of the family were farmers; today members of the Fairbanks family are found in all walks of life. Thaddeus Fairbanks of St. Johnsbury, Vermont, was the inventor of the standard scales which bear his name; another, Nathaniel Kellog Fairbanks, began life as an apprentice to a bricklayer in Wayne County, New York, ending it as a multi-millionaire in Chicago. Another descendant, Charles Warren Fairbanks, was the son of a Union County, Ohio, farmer and was born in a one-room log farmhouse. His father had migrated from New England. Charles Warren, in spite of poverty, worked his way through Ohio Wesleyan University, and graduated in the class of 1872. While working for the Associated Press he studied law at night; began practice in Indianapolis and quickly gained a national reputation as a railroad attorney. Chosen United States

Senator in 1897, he was elected Vice-President of the United States in 1904.

The family of Hamlin Garland furnishes another example of the migrating farmer of former generations. His grandparents, originating in Maine, moved to Wisconsin; his father moved to Minnesota; then to Iowa; and finally to South Dakota. The family of the historian, Frederick Jackson Turner, furnishes still another example of American immigration. The original American Turners came from England to Massachusetts, whence after several generations they began their westward march. First they came to Connecticut; thence, northward into Vermont and on into New York along the shore of Lake Champlain. After a pause, the family turned westward into Michigan, Wisconsin, and finally Nebraska.[1]

The first census of the United States, that of 1790, revealed that ninety-four per cent of the population of the country, at that time about four millions, were living in the original thirteen states. The census of 1820 showed that one-fourth of the total population was living beyond the western limits of the old seaboard states; by 1850 nearly half the population of the nation was living in regions outside the original thirteen. In 1850 one-third of the free people born in the four southern states—Virginia, North and South Carolina, and Georgia—were living outside the

---

[1] An excellent summary of the westward movement of population may be found in Edward Channing, *History of the United States* (New York, 1921), V, chapter ii, "The Westward March." To this chapter I am also indebted for the facts in the above paragraph.

state of their birth.[2] The movement of population from the New England states into the newer sections of the country perhaps exceeded that from the southern states. Between 1790 and 1820 it has been estimated that New England lost 800,000 by migration to the West. Not only was there a vast movement out of New England, but within New England the population was shifting from the farms to the industrial towns, particularly after 1820.[3] The richness of the contributions which New England made to the West is illustrated by the fact that one-third of the members of the constitutional convention of Wisconsin in 1846 were of New England birth, and another third came from those sections in New York that had been settled by New England people. One-third of the Iowa constitutional convention the same year was made up of men of New England birth.[4] John C. Calhoun is credited with the statement that he could recall the time when the natives of Connecticut, together with the graduates of Yale College in Congress, came within five of making a majority of that body—a commentary on the widespread diffusion of Connecticut people throughout the West.[5]

The Middle Atlantic states, the richest and most populous section in the nation, were also the melting pot for the new European immigration which began to enter the

---

[2] Channing, *op. cit.*, V, 49–50.

[3] For an excellent survey of the shifting of population in the United States from 1830 to 1850, see Frederick Jackson Turner, *The United States, 1830–1850* (New York, 1935), chapter iii, "New England"; chapter iv, "The Middle Atlantic States"; and chapter v, "The South Atlantic States."

[4] *Ibid.*, 50.

[5] *Ibid.*, 49.

country following the close of the War of 1812. As early as 1850 one-sixth of the population of this region was of foreign birth. The fact that New York and Pennsylvania were much richer in natural resources than were the New England states, and possessed much unoccupied land in their respective central and western sections, accounts for the somewhat lower emigration from these states into the newer regions.

Thus the same basic problems for religion, created by the settlement of the thirteen colonies from across the Atlantic in the seventeenth and eighteenth centuries, were present in the nineteenth century as a consequence of the vast immigration which filled in the continent from the Alleghenies to the Pacific. It is true, as Horace Bushnell has pointed out, that the immigrants to the West had many advantages over the immigrants who crossed the Atlantic. They did not go beyond the bounds of their own country; they did not forsake a history as did their fathers who crossed the sea. Their connection with the older sections of the country exerted appreciable effect upon them. Wherever they went within the bounds of this vast new country, they were Americans still. "The pioneer could look out from his log cabin on the western border, and feel the warmth of a distant nationality glowing around him." But in spite of these advantages "the first generation (in the West) can hardly be said to have lived. They let go life, threw it away, for the benefit of the generation to come after them. . . . Whatever man or family removed to any new country . . . made a large remove . . . toward barbarism."

"Revivalism in America soared to its heights and plumbed its depths," as religion attempted to follow the ever-increasing stream of settlers across the Allegheny Mountains into the border lands of Kentucky, Tennessee, and Ohio, "the strategic battle ground of religion in the westward march of the nation." [6]

I

In the period of the Revolution, and in the years immediately following, religious and moral conditions of the country as a whole reached the lowest ebb tide in the entire history of the American people. And it was in the very midst of this period of moral and religious depression that the great western migration began.

It was soon found that the moral and religious forces best fitted to cope with the problems presented by the vast new western movement of population were those which had been forged in the colonial revivals by the Presbyterians, the Congregationalists, the Baptists, and the Methodists. Fortunately for the future of the great West and for the future of the country as a whole, these fully-organized religious bodies were already waiting and equipped to carry forward the battle for decency and religion in the great new West.

If morals and religion were at low ebb in the older settled seaboard regions, what could be expected in the newer, ruder sections west of the mountains? There they were cut

[6] Grover C. Loud, *Evangelized America* (New York, 1928), 95. This is a serious attempt to portray the part played by Revivalism in American history, but is often inaccurate.

off from the restraints and the refining influences of the
old home community with its church and school, and its
strict observance of the Sabbath. One missionary reporting
from the Western Reserve of Ohio in 1826, a region settled largely by Connecticut people, observed that the people of the region though coming from "a land of Bibles
and sabbaths and ministers and churches," "now act like
freed prisoners." They find themselves in a country "where
they can fight against God without fearing man." In New
England they walked the courts of God's house; "they deny
Christ in this land of sinful liberty." [1]

The greatest single curse of the whole country at this
period, and especially of the raw frontier, was home-made
whiskey. It was considered on the frontier almost as much
of a necessity as bread and meat. Everybody indulged—
men, women, and children, preachers and church members,
as well as the ungodly. Stores had open kegs of whiskey
with cups attached for all to help themselves. It was freely
served at all the social gatherings, log rollings, corn husk-
ings and house raisings. At the loading of flatboats there
was always a keg of whiskey on the bank with head knocked
off and a gourd ready. As a sad consequence of the abundance of the fiery liquid, a large section of frontier society
was debauched and whiskey-sodden. Of all the many cases
of church discipline to be found in frontier church records, drunkenness was by far the most common single
cause.

---

[1] W. W. Sweet, "The Churches as Moral Courts of the Frontier,"
Church History (March, 1933), 3-21.

II

It is a significant fact that what is often called the second Great Awakening, which came in the latter years of the eighteenth and the early years of the nineteenth centuries, started as a Presbyterian movement. It began in two little backwoods colleges, Hampden-Sidney and Washington, both in Virginia. They, together with Jefferson College in Western Pennsylvania (founded in 1801), furnished a good share of the revivalistic Presbyterian leadership in the early West. All of them had been founded by the Presbyterians to train a ministry for the Church, but the deadness in religion which characterized the entire nation during and following the Revolution affected them until the year 1786. In that year a great religious concern began to take hold of the students at Hampden-Sidney College, largely engendered by the students themselves. The revival spread to Washington College. Out of these college revivals came some of the most influential leaders in American Presbyterianism in the next generation. Not a few of them became educational leaders of prominence, such as James Blythe, an early President of Transylvania University, and Archibald Alexander, later to become president of Hampden-Sidney and professor of theology at Princeton. But their principal significance lies in the fact that they trained a ministry for the new West over the Alleghenies. The Presbyterian revivalists thus were, as a rule, men who had been college trained—a fact that has a significant bearing on the different strains of revivalism which soon began to appear on the frontier.

The Congregational phase of the Second Awakening likewise had its center in the colleges, particularly at Yale. It is true, what were termed "outpourings of the Holy Spirit" were reported at various places in Connecticut, and from other places throughout Congregationaldom, from 1797 onward; [1] but the revival at Yale under the leadership of President Timothy Dwight soon took on a national significance. For, what Hampden-Sidney, Washington, Jefferson, and Princeton colleges were for Presbyterianism, Yale and Andover particularly were for the Congregationalists—training schools for revivalists. It was but natural, therefore, that Yale and Princeton colleges furnished the pattern for practically all the early frontier colleges.

The Presbyterians from the start were more influential in the West than were the Congregationalists, and both were more or less limited in their appeal. The Presbyterian preacher on a missionary tour was largely concerned in finding those localities where people of Presbyterian background were settled, and it was these people who formed the nucleus around which a church would eventually be formed. In other words, the Presbyterian missionary went forth looking for Presbyterians, and Presbyterianism always prospered best where there were to be found Presbyterian settlers. It was very rare indeed that a Presbyterian congregation in the West would be formed of the raw material of the frontier; seldom was it constituted of a cross-section of western society. The Congregational missionary to the

---

[1] Charles R. Keller, *The Second Great Awakening in Connecticut* (New Haven, 1942), chapter iii, "Counter-Reformation," 36–69.

West likewise confined his work in a large measure to New England immigrants. This fact greatly limited the effectiveness of both these bodies in the West, and helps to account for their relatively small numbers as compared to the Baptists and the Methodists.[2]

Not only did the Presbyterians limit their appeal to a relatively small section of frontier society, but they were also handicapped by the rigidity of their creed and polity. It was soon discovered by some of the leaders among the western Presbyterians that frequently the revivalist preachers were "loose in doctrine," and some of the Presbyterian revivalists were accused of even accepting "the doctrines of grace as held by the Methodists" and otherwise diluting "the excellent standards" of the Confession of Faith. Thus Richard McNemar, a revivalist Presbyterian preacher who left the Church and became a Shaker, describes the position of the anti-revivalists among the Presbyterians:

The people among whom the revival began, were generally Calvinists; and although they had been long praying in words, for the outpouring of the Spirit; and believed that God had "foreordained whatsoever comes to pass, yet, when it came to pass that their prayer was answered, and the spirit began to flow like many waters from a cloud of witnesses; and souls were convicted of sin and cried for mercy and found hope and comfort in the news of a Saviour; they rose up and quarreled

---

[2] For a discussion of this whole matter see W. W. Sweet, *Religion on the American Frontier: The Presbyterians* (New York, 1936), chapter iii, "The Presbyterians in the Early West"; also *Religion on the American Frontier: The Congregationalists* (Chicago, 1939), chapter ii, "The Plan of Union."

with the work, because it did not come to pass that the subjects of it were willing to adopt their soul-stupefying creed." [3]

The camp meeting likewise originated among western
Presbyterians, and the most spectacular one ever held, that
at Cane Ridge, Kentucky, in August 1801, was organized
under their leadership. The first great Presbyterian frontier
revivalist in the West was James McGready, and it was as
a result of the drawing power of his revivalistic preaching
that the camp meeting movement was inaugurated. So
large were the numbers which attended his meetings in
Logan County, Kentucky, it was found necessary to hold
them out-of-doors. And due to the fact that so many came
from great distances, they were compelled to remain over
night, with the result that not a few came prepared to
remain several days. Some came in wagons fitted up for
temporary lodging; others built shelters of brush. The first
planned camp meeting was held in Logan County, Kentucky, in July 1800, to which invitations were sent by
McGready throughout the whole back-woods country. As
a result, a great concourse of people assembled from as far
away as forty, fifty, and even a hundred miles. A regular
encampment was laid out in the form of a hollow square,
and the interior fitted up for worship, with parallel rows
of hewn logs designed as seats, and a preaching stand in
the center. Some people came with tents, but a majority
slept in their wagons. Such was the origin of the camp

---

[3] Richard McNemar, *The Kentucky Revival: or A Short History of the
Late Extraordinary Outpouring of the Spirit of God in the Western States
of America* (Cincinnati, 1807); reprinted (New York, 1846), 27.

meeting. Once inaugurated, the movement spread like wildfire throughout the length and breadth of the frontier.

Robert Davidson, the historian of Presbyterianism in Kentucky, thus pictures the tremendous appeal of the camp meeting to frontier society. So great were the numbers of those attending these outdoor assemblies that:

The woods and paths seemed alive with people, and the number reported as attending is almost incredible. The laborer quitted his task; Age snatched his crutch; Youth forgot his pastime; the plow was left in the furrow; the deer enjoyed a respite upon the mountains; business of all kinds was suspended; dwelling houses were deserted; whole neighborhoods were emptied; bold hunters and sober matrons, young women and maidens, and little children, flocked to the common center of attraction; every difficulty was surmounted, every risk ventured, to be present at the camp meeting.[4]

The great Cane Ridge camp meeting in Bourbon County in August, 1801, is the dividing point in western Presbyterianism. Barton W. Stone was the Presbyterian minister most responsible for this spectacular gathering. It was a general camp meeting and people of all denominations attended. The numerous contemporary accounts all agree in the vast multitudes on the grounds and the awe-inspiring effects produced. One of the oldest and most reliable of the Presbyterian ministers in attendance stated that during the course of the meeting the number who fell was about

---

[4] Robert Davidson, *History of the Presbyterian Church in the State of Kentucky:* with a preliminary Sketch of the Churches in the Valley of Virginia (New York, 1848), 136–137.

3,000. The "falling exercise" was generally considered a clear manifestation of the power of God working on the hearts of people. The other exercises which agitated hundreds, as jerking, rolling, dancing, and barking, were looked upon as dubious, to say the least. Throughout it all—the meeting lasted for several days—there was constant noise and confusion. Many who attended were dissolute and irreligious characters, and they outnumbered by far those who came with religious intent. There was much drinking of raw whiskey plentifully supplied by hucksters from wagons on the outskirts of the campgrounds. To those accustomed to quietness, dignity, and order in worship such confusion was, of course, most distasteful and many looked upon it as a travesty on religion.[5]

From this time forward western Presbyterianism sharply divided over the camp meeting and revivalism, and the controversy which ensued between those who favored and those who opposed them soon resulted in division. One division centered in the Cumberland Presbytery which by 1810 had developed into the Cumberland Presbyterian Church. Another centered in northern Kentucky from the influences coming out of the Cane Ridge meeting and eventually developed into a definite schism known as the New Light or Stonite which was to become a wing of the Disciples body. Both schismatic groups repudiated Calvinism and championed the emotional type of appeal. This

---

[5] W. W. Sweet, *Religion on the American Frontier: The Presbyterians,* 86–90, for a summary of the camp meeting influence on frontier Presbyterianism.

did not mean that those who opposed the camp meeting excesses were also opposed to revivals. But it did mean that from this time forward the regular Presbyterians put the stamp of approval only upon a particular kind of revivalism.[6] To the Presbyterians and Congregationalists, now working together in the West, under the Plan of Union of 1801, a genuine revival was one where there was "no wildness and extravagance" and "very little commotion of the animal feelings," and where "the word of God distils upon the mind like the gentle rain, and the Holy Spirit comes down like the dew, diffusing a blessed influence on all around." [7]

To bring about a real work of the spirit, according to Archibald Alexander, professor of theology at Princeton, "the gospel must be preached in its purity" and to people who "have been well instructed in the doctrines of Christianity." By this, of course, he meant that the doctrines of Calvinism were the only pure doctrines. He admits that the Methodists, Cumberland Presbyterians, and Baptists have carried on revivals, but they preach a gospel in which much error is mingled with evangelical truth, and the "baleful effects of the error . . . will be sure to be manifest"; it is like mingling poisonous ingredients "with wholesome foods." The above, I think, is a fair statement of what

---

[6] This is brought out clearly in the letters found in the Appendix of W. B. Sprague, *Lectures on Revivals of Religion* (New York, 1833). Davenport terms the two types of revivalism the rational and the emotional. F. M. Davenport, *Primitive Traits in Religious Revivals* (New York, 1905), especially chapter xiii, "The Personal and the Rational in Religion."

[7] From the letter of Archibald Alexander, Sprague, *op. cit.*, 231–232.

might be called "Presbyterian-Congregational revivalism."
But such revivalism could only take place, according to
Alexander, among a people who have been carefully
taught by catechizing, and who have been instructed in
"the truths of the Bible." What was to be done religiously
for the great mass of the people who had not had and
could not have careful instruction in the great truths of
the Bible, and who had not been under catechetical instruction, he does not indicate. And this is where the
Baptists, the Methodists, the Disciples, and the Cumberland Presbyterians enter the revivalistic scene.[8]

It is a significant fact that the Presbyterian-Congregational type of revivalism produced the most outstanding
revivalists. Throughout the eighteenth century this type of
revivalism was stressed by Presbyterians and Congregationalists and the most distinguished ministers of both
Churches were revivalistic in their preaching. This was
particularly true of Lyman Beecher. His principal purpose
in life was the promotion of revivals and he attacked any
and all who in any way hindered or opposed them. His best
friend, Nathaniel W. Taylor, the first professor of theology

---

[8] In a letter written to the Secretaries of the American Home Missionary
Society in September, 1846, by a missionary from Benton County, Arkansas,
the work of the several religious bodies at work in that region is appraised.
Cumberland Presbyterians, Campbellites, Baptists, and Methodists are all
lumped together as "standing in the way" of the Society, and he concludes
that "After a minute examination and mature and prayerful deliberation
I have come to the settled conviction that it would be decidedly for the
religious interests of Arkansas if every minister and preacher of the above
denominations were out of the State." He acknowledges that they do save
some souls, "But the souls are saved at too great an expense." (Sweet,
Presbyterians, op. cit., 695–700.)

at Yale Divinity School, was a revivalistic preacher before
he became a teacher of theology, and "all his theology was
shaped and framed with reference to the doctrine and work
of the conversion of sinners to God." [9] The generations of
students who sat under him were both indoctrinated with
his theology and imbued with the same purpose. Perhaps
a typical evangelist of this type was Asahel Nettleton, a
contemporary of Taylor's and Beecher's. He gave his life
to evangelism, never held a permanent pulpit and never
asked remuneration for his services. There was nothing ex-
ceptional in his preaching except the simplicity and searching nature of it. To his pulpit ministrations he added
house-to-house visitation and personal conference, and his
converts were always thoroughly schooled in the fundamental teaching of Christianity. He was opposed to the
more liberal Calvinism of Taylor and Beecher, and identified himself with the body of New England ministers who
established what is now Hartford Theological Seminary.

Revivalism found some adherents among Lutherans, the
German Reformed, and even among the Episcopalians.
Manross states that the Episcopal revivals differed from
those of the more evangelical bodies in degree rather than
in kind, as the Episcopalian Evangelicals "were more careful than others to guard against emotional extravagance,"
and "seldom took an active part in community revivals." [10]
In the German Reformed Church revivalism brought on a

---

[9] Sidney E. Mead, *Nathaniel William Taylor, Connecticut Liberal*
(Chicago, 1942), 158.
[10] W. W. Manross, *The Episcopal Church in the United States, 1800–
1840* (New York, 1938), 104-105.

controversy in which Dr. John W. Nevin, president of Mercersburg Theological Seminary, took the leading part. In a little book published in 1843 entitled *The Anxious Bench*, Nevin discriminated between "Genuine" and "Spurious" revivals, contending that a true revival must grow out of the life of the Church, and cannot be forcibly brought about from without and by mechanical means.[11]

III

As has been already indicated, the Presbyterian-Congregational type of revivalism of the first half of the eighteenth century made only a limited appeal. It was a type of revivalism which was based on Calvinistic doctrines; the kind of revivalism which swept the frontier was Arminian, in emphasis. The first offered salvation to the few; the second offered it to all. The former was aristocratic; the latter democratic.

The great protagonists of frontier revivalism were the Baptists and the Methodists. Each pursued their own way in carrying on their work, but both were effective in bringing the gospel of repentance to the common man. Until the formation of the Baptist Home Mission Society in 1832 the Baptist work on the frontier was carried on almost entirely by the farmer-preacher. The pattern for this type of ministry was found in the Baptist phase of the Virginia

---

[11] See Theodore Apple, *The Life and Work of John Williamson Nevin* (Philadelphia, 1889). Also article on "Nevin" in *Dictionary of American Biography*, XIII.

and North Carolina revivals. It was largely an unsalaried and an uneducated ministry, that is, uneducated as far as the schools were concerned. It was a devoted and self-sacrificing ministry, but with an extremely limited outlook, as the anti-mission movement among frontier Baptists which began about 1820 indicates. Unlike the Methodists, the frontier Baptists had no conception of the world as their parish. The great bulk of the frontier Baptists preached a modified Calvinism, while their form of Church government was a pure democracy, a fact that undoubtedly gave them a large popularity in frontier society.

By the eighteen-twenties the whole settled portion of the West was covered with a network of Baptist Associations, which were voluntary organizations made up of Baptist churches. The meetings of these Associations corresponded somewhat to the camp meetings. It became the custom to hold them in the woods where the general public was invited, and it was not uncommon for many thousands to be in attendance. [1]

As a frontier religious force the Methodists were undoubtedly the most successful, if success is to be judged by the numbers that were reached by the Methodist gospel. When the regular Presbyterians threw overboard the camp meeting, the Methodists appropriated it, and made it, to a large degree, a Methodist institution. Bishop Asbury makes frequent references to camp meetings in his *Journal*. On

---

[1] W. W. Sweet, *Religion on the American Frontier: The Baptists* (New York, 1931), especially chapter iii, "The Frontier Baptist Preacher and the Frontier Baptist Church."

December 12, 1805, he remarks that "my northern letters" have brought news of many successful camp meetings:

> . . . at Duck Creek camp-meeting five hundred souls; at Accomack camp-meeting, four hundred; at Annamessex chapel, in the woods, two hundred; at Somerset, Line chapel, one hundred and twenty; at Todd's chapel, Dorset, two hundred; at Carolina quarterly meeting, seventy-five; all, all these profess to have received converting grace.[2]

The following year (November 9, 1806) he records the receipt of a letter giving an account of the Long-Calm camp meeting in Maryland. It lasted from the eighth to the fourteenth of October, and:

> Five hundred and eighty were said to be converted and one hundred and twenty believers confirmed and sanctified. Lord, let this work be general!

In August 1808, he notes that at a camp meeting on Deer Creek in Ohio "there were twenty-three traveling and local preachers on the ground," about a hundred and twenty-five tents and wagons, and about two thousand people.[3] In November of the same year he exclaims:

> . . . great news from Georgia, South and North Carolina! Thirty, or forty or fifty souls converted at camp-meetings; but in old Virginia the work is still greater. . . .

In August 1809 he remarks:[4]

---

[2] Vol. III, 210–211.
[3] *Ibid.*, III, 286.
[4] *Ibid.*, III, 316.

"We must attend to camp-meetings, they make our harvest time." The same year in the Miami district there were seventeen camp meetings; in Scioto circuit there were four; "in Hockhocking two; Deer Creek two; Mad River three; White Water two; Cincinnati two; and White two." [5] And a few days later he states: "More of camp-meetings—I hear and see the great effects produced by them, and this year there will be more than ever." [6]

The evidence furnished by Bishop Asbury's *Journal* alone is sufficient to show the great importance of the camp meeting in frontier Methodism. There is, however, a great abundance of other contemporary evidence. This is doubtless one of the principal reasons why the camp meeting has been overemphasized. Many who have written of frontier religion have given chief attention to the spectacular and the unusual. They have assumed that the camp meeting represented about all there was of religious influence and activity in the West. Yet, as a matter of fact, the camp meeting was never recognized as an official Methodist institution. There was never any legislation concerning it; the name *camp meeting* does not occur in any of the General Conference *Indices*. There are no rules in the *Discipline* to govern it. It was widely used, but always as an extra occasion in the economy of Methodism. Preachers never answered any formal questions concerning it in the Quarterly Conference. Gradually there grew up certain ideas as to how camp meetings could best be organized and

---

[5] *Ibid.*, III, 321.
[6] *Ibid.*, III. See Index for numerous other references.

regulated, and camp meeting manuals came into circulation, but none of them was ever officially adopted by any church body.[7]

There has been entirely too much stress placed upon the emotional excesses of camp meetings and all too little upon the routine work of the frontier churches and preachers. All the more aggressive frontier churches stressed the necessity of conversion, and all of them had their own way of helping to bring it about. All were intensely individualistic in their dealings with their members and exercised rigid disciplinary oversight over them. Among the Presbyterians only those who were properly qualified were permitted to partake of the sacrament. A communion sermon was first preached to be followed by what was called *fencing of the tables*. This was an exercise in which each member was examined and if any were found guilty of breaking any of the ten commandments they were debarred. Those who were qualified were given small lead disks, called *tokens*, which were collected by the elders

[7] See editorial article in the *Western Christian Advocate* (August 15. 1834). The following heads are discussed in the article: *Best time to hold* camp-meetings—last of July to last of September; *Place*, where there is good water, dry ground, pleasant shade, agreeable woods for walking and recreation, timber for tent poles and fire wood, and pasturage for horses; *Entertainment* to be provided for each individual before he arrives; *Rules* to be devised for regulating the temporal concerns; *Civil Law* to be strictly enforced, especially against selling liquor within a mile of the camp, and all hucksters to be driven from the ground; *Camp-meeting* to be held less frequently—instead of one or more for each circuit each year, there should be only two or three for each district; *Religious exercises*—sermons short, especially when there are several in the course of a day, sacraments to be administered according to the usual formulas, no extravagant exercises of any kind and meetings should not be continued until late at night.

after the communicants had seated themselves at the tables. This was a period of self-examination and was undoubtedly effective in helping to maintain high standards of life and conduct.[8]

The frontier Baptist Churches held monthly congregational meetings at which all members were required to be present. It was here that the life of each member came under the scrutiny of the Church. It was the duty of each member to watch over the conduct of fellow members and to bring charges against anyone guilty of any infraction of the rules of Christian conduct or church order. Indeed a good share of the business of these congregational meetings was devoted to the hearing of charges, and unrepentant members were excluded without fear or favor. Intoxication was the most frequent cause for church discipline, though such things as adultery, unchristian business dealing, gambling, immoral conduct, stealing, removing landmarks, tale-bearing, quarreling, dishonest horse trading, cruelty to slaves, misusing wives, are some of the other causes.[9]

The Methodist system of dealing with individual members was through the Class meeting. Every Methodist member was assigned to a Class and was thus placed under the direct supervision of a Class Leader. Once a week each Class met when each member was called upon to stand on

[8] For an account of the Presbyterian communion practices see W. W. Sweet, Presbyterians, op. cit., 63–64. See also G. A. MacLennan, The Story of the Old Time Communion Service, etc. (Toronto, 1924).

[9] See W. W. Sweet, Religion on the American Frontier: The Baptists (New York, 1931); consult Index under Discipline. See also W. W. Sweet, "The Churches as Moral Courts of the Frontier," Church History (March, 1933).

his feet and give of his experience. Each member in good standing was given a Class ticket and no one was permitted to partake of the Sacrament of the Lord's Supper who did not possess his ticket. Thus, in all the principal frontier churches, religion was highly individualized.

Frontier religion was also much more solidly based than is usually pictured. The long lists of catechisms, Bibles, testaments, hymn books, disciplines, and other religious books, which were sold by the Methodist circuit riders to the people on their circuits are evidence of the religious instructions afforded.[10] The fact that almost all the early Presbyterian preachers in the West were also school teachers is evidence that theirs was a teaching as well as a preaching ministry.

IV

A third type of revivalism made its appearance on the frontier when Charles G. Finney began his ministry in Jefferson County, central western New York in 1824. The two little frontier towns to which he had been assigned as Presbyterian missionary, Evans Mills and Antwerp, were rough, uncouth communities, but immediately under the vivid preaching of the ex-lawyer-preacher a wave of revivalism began to sweep through the whole region. He preached out-of-doors; in barns; in schoolhouses. Thus began one of the most remarkable careers in the history of modern revivalists. Converted under Presbyterian auspices, Finney

---

[10] See the book lists in the *Benjamin Lakin Papers* (MSS. University of Chicago Collection).

from the start rejected the Calvinistic doctrine of Predestination and insisted that salvation was for all. In spite of such "heresy" in Presbyterian eyes, he was ordained by a lenient Presbytery and from then onward pursued his own independent way both theologically and otherwise. He showed disregard for denominational lines at a time when they were closely drawn, and his revivalistic methods, called by his enemies the "new measures," though bringing results, soon precipitated trouble.

As the Finney revival (1824–1827) swept through northern New York, moved eastward through the older sections of the state, and neared the Hudson River and the borders of New England, the Congregational and Presbyterian leaders in that section began to be concerned lest Finney revivalism, with its *new measures*, would enter New England. The stanch Calvinist revivalist Asahel Nettleton, and the semi-Calvinist Lyman Beecher, planned a meeting with Finney near Albany, in order to come to some agreement as to the proper way to conduct revivals. So completely did Finney disarm them, however, that a little later Beecher and Nettleton headed a committee to invite Finney to hold a great revival in Boston. Finney now became a national figure and demands for his services came from all directions.

The *new measures* which had so aroused the conservative revivalists was his practice of inviting people under conviction to come forward and occupy what came to be called "the anxious bench"; of praying for people by name in public meetings, especially in cottage prayer meetings which would be held throughout the community where the revival was in progress; in permitting women to pray in public and in the presence of men, and of using what was termed "undignified means" of advertising his meetings.[1] His doctrine of *perfectionism*, only hinted at in his early preaching, came to full flower in his later preaching and in his teaching of theology at Oberlin. When he came to Oberlin College in 1836 as professor of theology, he brought with him a great tent in which to hold meetings, and at the top of the center pole supporting the tent was a large streamer upon which was written in large letters, "Holiness to the Lord."

As Finney came more and more to approximate the Methodist theology, he more and more came under the criticism of the Calvinists. In his lectures on Revivals of Religion, delivered at the Broadway Tabernacle in 1835, Finney had this to say:

Look at the Methodists. Many of their ministers are unlearned, in the common sense of the term, many of them taken

---

[1] According to Finney's own statement (*Memoirs* (New York, 1876), p. 135), the doctrines stressed in his early revivals were: "The total moral, voluntary depravity of unregenerate man; the necessity of a radical change of heart, through the truth, by the agency of the Holy Ghost; the divinity and humanity of our Lord Jesus Christ; his vicarious atonement, equal to the wants of all mankind; the gift, divinity and agency of the Holy Ghost; repentance, faith, justification by faith, sanctification by faith, persistence in holiness as a condition of salvation. . . ."

Finney's method of preaching has been described as follows: He 'pressed the anxious sinners with the closely reasoned truth." And only after he had won their minds did he address himself to their "sympathy." "Even then he exercised his gift of hypnotic eloquence with moderation, and never for a moment did he let the emotions of his converts get beyond his iron will."

right from the shop or the farm, and yet they have gathered congregations . . . and won souls everywhere. Wherever the Methodists have gone, their plain, pointed and simple, but warm and animated mode of preaching has always gathered congregations. Few Presbyterians ministers have gathered so large assemblies or won so many souls. Now are we to be told that we must pursue the same old, formal mode of doing things, amidst all these changes?. . . It is impossible that the public mind should be held by such preaching. We must have exciting, powerful preaching, or the devil will have the people, except what the Methodists can save. . . . Many ministers are finding it out already, that a Methodist preacher, without the advantages of a liberal education, will draw a congregation around him which a Presbyterian minister, with perhaps ten times as much learning, cannot equal, because he has not the earnest manner of the other, and does not pour out fire upon his hearers when he preaches.[2]

This was hard for the Presbyterians and the Presbyterianized Congregationalists to take, while the Methodists came more and more to his support. As a consequence, Oberlin graduates going into the ministry were not welcomed either by the Presbyterians or Congregationalists. At a convention held in Cleveland, of which Lyman Beecher was the prime mover, to consider the support of western colleges Oberlin representatives were barred. In 1840 two young men, brothers, both later to become dis-

---

[2] Charles G. Finney, *Lectures on Revivals of Religion* (2d ed.; New York, 1835), 252–253. For an excellent summary of Finney's developing theology see M. E. Gaddis, *Christian Perfectionism in America* (typed Ph.D. thesis, University of Chicago, 1929, 313–334).

tinguished ministers, were denied licenses by the Huron Presbytery because they were Oberlin graduates and refused to declare that they did not believe "in the doctrines taught at Oberlin and in their way of doing things." [3] Other Presbyteries took like action. Oberlin men were rigidly excluded from early Wisconsin by the Presbyterian-Congregational Union. But in spite of this hostility Oberlin carried on under Finney's leadership, and by the eighteen-fifties had achieved a national and international reputation. It is an interesting fact that David Livingstone sent his younger brother from Scotland to Oberlin, where he graduated in 1845. [4]

Thus the Finney type of revivalism came to occupy a position midway between the Congregational-Presbyterian revivalism on the right and the Baptist-Methodist revivalism on the left. And of all the types of revivalism, it exercised the largest influence in raising up leaders of reform. Many of the early students at Oberlin were drawn from among Finney's converts, especially from central and western New York, the region where his influence was most deeply imbedded. This section became known as the "burnt region" because of the many waves of revivalism which swept over it; and this fact helps to account for the

---

[3] Gaddis, *op. cit.*, 327–328, 333–334. Albert T. Swing, *James Harris Fairchild or Sixty-eight years with a Christian College* (New York, 1907), 108. See also W. W. Sweet, *Religion on the American Frontier: The Congregationalists* (Chicago, 1939), 20, 36. See also Robert Samuel Fletcher, *A History of Oberlin College,* etc. (2 vols.) (Oberlin, Ohio, 1943), I, 14–16, 207–235.

[4] W. W. Sweet, *Makers of Christianity* (New York, 1937), 265. Fletcher, *op. cit.*, II, 540–543.

many new and strange religious developments which took place in that region.

V

As the nineteenth century wore on, the differences between the several types of revivalism became less and less distinct. Educational and cultural differences between the major American Churches, so conspicuous at the beginning of the nineteenth century, by its end had largely disappeared. Likewise, theological differences were more and more watered down and in this leveling-off process distinctions between the types of revivalism tended to grow less. Thus by the time Dwight L. Moody and the succession of professional revivalists came upon the scene in the latter nineteenth and early twentieth centuries, all the revivalistic Churches were ready to unit in the support of their great interdenominational evangelistic campaigns which were so characteristic of the period.[1]

---

[1] W. W. Sweet, "Rapprochement in American Protestantism," *Religion in Life,* XI, No. 1. Winter Number, 1941–1942, 74–83.

CHAPTER SEVEN

THE BY-PRODUCTS OF REVIVALISM

REVIVALISM has been a major influence in American social history. This, I think, no present-day social historian would deny. Its primary influence, however, has been in the realm of personal religion; within the lives of men and women. Such an influence is, of course, impossible to assess accurately. It has raised moral standards in countless communities throughout the land; it has affected reforms in life and manners; it has enabled religion to reach down to the lowest levels of society and thereby time without number has rendered less sodden the great unleavened masses of men. It has served to enlarge the membership of the churches, of all denominations, and greatly increased the impact of religion on American life. These are some of the direct results of revivalism. The purpose of this chapter is to attempt to assess the more or less indirect influences of revivalism—or, in other words, we plan here to look at some of its by-products.

I

Revivalism has not been a one-hundred-per cent asset to religion. Indeed, in not a few instances it has been the cause of unfortunate consequences.

Among the chief of these has been controversy and division. Revivalism, in fact, has been one of the most divisive

factors in organized religion in America. In every one of
the several phases of the colonial revivals, controversy and
division resulted. The revival among the Dutch churches
in New Jersey under Theodore J. Frelinghuysen's leadership, as has already been noted, divided the Dutch ministers and churches in America into two warring camps; and
the bitterness engendered, especially on the part of the
anti-revivalists, bore little resemblance to that meek spirit
which the New Testament enjoins. The Log College revival divided colonial Presbyterianism into two hostile divisions, the New Side and the Old Side. In the famous sermon by Gilbert Tennent on the "Danger of an Unconverted Ministry," he described those who resisted the
revival as "moral negroes" who hinder instead of help
others "in at the straight gate," and stated that they resembled the Pharisees of Christ's day "as one crow's egg
does another." On the other hand, the anti-revivalists pro-
tested "the heterodox and anarchical principles of Tennent
and his followers, and declared that they had "no right to
be acknowledged as members of any judicatory of Christ."
Their protest ends with, "Let God arise and let his enemies be scattered." Of all the controversies which arose
out of the colonial revivals, that in New England was the
most prolonged and the most disastrous in its consequences. Here theology was more involved than elsewhere,
and when that is the case there is small chance of healing
a schism. The net result was the permanent division of
New England Congregationalism, and a turmoil which
lasted for more than half a century.

The Second Awakening, or the great revival movement which swept the nation in the latter years of the eighteenth and early years of the nineteenth centuries, was even more divisive in its effects than the colonial revivals. The Presbyterians were the principal victims of division, especially those which arose as a result of frontier influences. The inelasticity of Presbyterian doctrine and polity was largely responsible for these unfortunate results. Any attempt to modify stiff-backed Calvinism of the Westminster Creed or the polity there embodied brought controversy and, eventually, schism. In fact, there were three distinct Presbyterian divisions which took place on the early frontier, all as a consequence of revivalism: The Cumberland Presbyterian schism; the New Light schism; and the Shaker schism. Interesting illustrations of the divisive effect of revivalism and other factors on frontier Presbyterianism were seen in the situation in Princeton, Illinois, and in Bloomington, Indiana. In the former town of a few thousand people, in the middle of the last century, there were eleven Presbyterian churches; in the latter town, at about the same time, there were eight.

The most able critic of colonial revivalism was the Rev. Charles Chauncy of First Church, Boston, the most influential Boston minister of his time. His arguments against revivalism, which appeared in his book *Seasonable Thoughts on the State of Religion in New England,* published in 1743, are an exhaustive summary of all the anti-revivalistic arguments which have been advanced from that day to this. He condemned the "censoriousness" of

the revivalists: their invading the parishes of other ministers uninvited, the practice of permitting uneducated persons to take upon themselves the preaching of the word of
God, and the confusions and tumults which accompanied
revivals. Revivalism also fostered doctrinal errors contrary
to the correct doctrines of the gospel. Another argument
advanced was that the practice of the revivalists holding
meetings on week-days took poor people away from their
work and thus encouraged shiftlessness, an indication that
the so-called "upper classes" were becoming fearful of
what revivalism might do to their privileged position.

The confusion and disorder which revivalism undoubtedly fostered, on the frontier, and especially in the camp
meeting, struck a blow at order and dignity in worship
from which the revivalistic churches have not yet fully
recovered. Often in camp meetings a dozen different
hymns or songs would be sung at once; and equally often,
as many prayers were being offered at the same time in
tones so loud that a stranger might infer that the one praying assumed that God was deaf. Another unfortunate influence coming out of revivalism was the type of religious
songs used, many of which were the crudest doggerel.
Because of the absence of hymn books, it was not uncommon for "spiritual songs" to be improvised on the spot. The
preacher would raise a tune, furnishing two lines and a
chorus; when the congregation had sung that, he would be
ready with two more lines, and so on more or less in-
definitely. A popular camp meeting song, found in a song-
book published in 1807, gives evidence of having had such

an origin. It is entitled, *Shout Old Satan's Kingdom Down.*
It begins:

> This day my soul has caught on fire, *Hallelujah!*
> I feel that heaven is coming nigher,
> > *O glory Hallelujah!*
>
> > *Chorus*
> Shout, shout, we're gaining ground, *Hallelujah!*
> We'll shout old Satan's kingdom down, *Hallelujah!*
> When Christians pray, the Devil runs, *Hallelujah!*
> And leaves the field to Zion's sons,
> > *O glory Hallelujah!*

and so on for eighteen verses.[1]

An extreme example of crudity is Hymn 107 in the
same compilation.

> The world, the devil and Tom Paine,
> Have tried their force, but all in vain,
> They can't prevail, the reason is,
> The Lord defends the Methodist.
>
> They pray, they sing, they preach the best,
> And do the Devil most molest,
> If Satan had his vicious way,
> He'd kill and damn them all today.
>
> They are despised by Satan's train,
> Because they shout and preach so plain,
> I'm bound to march in endless bliss,
> And die a shouting Methodist.

---

[1] *Hymns and Spiritual Songs,* compiled by Stith Mead (Richmond, 1807). Also *The New and Improved Camp Meeting Hymn Book,* etc., by Orange Scott (3d ed.) (Brookfield, Mass., 1832).

Revivalism has been responsible for over-emphasizing the emotional and underestimating the rational element in religious experience. Too often even today the ministers of revivalistic Churches entirely overlook, or at least largely neglect, their teaching function. Their people are not well grounded in the great Christian truths. They have come into the Church on the basis of an emotional experience, and when that emotional experience cools off there is little if anything left. To use Davenport's words, "It becometh not religion to disparage reason. She owes too great a debt to it. . . . Christianity has never been simply emotional fervor, much less . . . fanaticism or superstition." [2] On the other hand, religion is more than reason and intellect; it is fundamentally a great emotion and a plan of life. Most of our great decisions are made emotionally. In certain realms of life, emotion is a better guide than reason. And that is true in the higher realms more frequently than in the lower. Our homes are built on the basis of a great emotion; men and women undertake the great sacrificial duties of life carried forward by a great emotion.

Errors of thought are as frequent and profound as errors of emotion. Borden P. Bowne thus criticizes a purely emotional religion. Though Christianity is the religion of love, he says, yet love is more than a great emotion, for it "abides in the will rather than in the feeling," and its "distinguishing mark consists in the set purpose to please and to serve." [3] We cannot live a rounded Christian life without

---

[2] Davenport, *op. cit.*, 275.
[3] Borden P. Bowne, *The Christian Life* (New York, 1899), 92. See also comments by Davenport, *op. cit.*, 265–266.

both reason and emotion; they go hand in hand and both are necessary in the development of the higher life.

Lest I leave the impression that the camp meeting songs were generally of this latter type, quotations from some of the more dignified will help remedy that idea. One of the common experiences of the Methodist itinerant was the frequent change of circuits, and the necessity of saying farewell to faithful people, since one year was the time limit a preacher could serve in the early nineteenth century. The hymn entitled *The Minister's Farewell* must have been familiar to both the minister and people, and no doubt was often sung as the closing hymn of Annual Conferences.

> Farewell, my brethren in the Lord,
> The Gospel sounds the jubilee;
> My stammering tongue shall sound aloud,
> From land to land, from sea to sea;
>> And as I preach from place to place,
>> I'll trust alone in God's free grace.
>
> Farewell, in bonds of union dear,
> Like strings you twine about my heart;
> I humbly beg your earnest prayer,
> Till we shall meet no more to part,
>> Till we shall meet in worlds above,
>> Encircled in eternal love.[4]

The following hymn was doubtless a favorite with which to open the Class meeting.

[4] *The New and Improved Camp Meeting Hymn Book*, etc., *ibid.*, Hymn 56.

Come, my brethren, let us try,
    For a little season;
Every burden to lay by,
    Come and let us reason.

What is this that casts you down,
    What is this that grieves you?
Speak and let the worst be known,
    Speaking may relieve you.[5]

II

Strange as it may seem to those who think of revivalism only in terms of ignorance, superstition, and an exaggerated emotionalism, there is a very close relationship between the history of higher education in America and revivalism.

Of the nine colonial colleges, the six established between 1740 and 1769—Pennsylvania, Princeton, Columbia, Rutgers, Brown, and Dartmouth—had some relationship either directly or indirectly to the great colonial awakenings. Previous to the colonial revivals, only the two established Churches—the Congregationalist and the Episcopalian—had founded colleges. None of the dissenter bodies were numerous enough to support a college until the revivals had increased their numbers, nor could they have done so except in the Middle Colonies and Rhode Island where there were no established Churches. The College of New Jersey, or Princeton, was the child of the Presbyterian revivalists and was established in 1746, the very year William Tennent's Log College was closed as a

---

[5] *Ibid.*, Hymn 68.

result of its founder's death. Princeton's first five presidents
—Jonathan Dickinson, Aaron Burr, Jonathan Edwards,
Samuel Davies, and Samuel Finley—were all outstanding
revivalist preachers. George Whitefield's part in the establishment of colleges in colonial America furnishes an interesting chapter in the history of the beginnings of higher
education in this country. He was the indirect founder of
the College of Philadelphia, and was an important influence in the founding of Princeton and Dartmouth. He did
his best also to turn his Georgia Orphanage into a college,
and it was the refusal of the King's Privy Council to permit
him to establish it on an interdenominational basis, as he
desired, which caused him to abandon the enterprise.[1]

The influence of the Second Great Awakening upon
the establishment of colleges is also easily discernible.
Naturally many young men who had experienced conversion in the great revivals felt the call to the ministry. To
carry out that desire meant educational preparation; that in
turn meant the establishment of academies and colleges to
meet the increased demand for an educated ministry. The
requirement in Presbyterian law that all candidates for the
ministry must have a diploma of Bachelor or Master of
Arts from a college or university, or at least a testimonial
of having gone through a regular course of study, meant
that the Presbyterians were the first to feel the demand

---

[1] See *The Works of the Reverend George Whitefield*, 6 vols. (London,
1770–72), III, 480–482, 573–575. Also W. W. Sweet, "Pennsylvania Men
and the Church," in *The General Magazine and Historical Chronicle* (University of Pennsylvania: The General Alumni Society, April, 1942), 348–
357.

for colleges in the West. How they met that demand is indicated by the fact that of the forty colleges and universities established in the United States from 1780 to 1830, in all sections of the country, thirteen were established by Presbyterians, four by Congregationalists, one by Congregationalists and Presbyterians in co-operation, six by Episcopalians, one by Catholics, three by Baptists, and one by the German Reformed and eleven by the states. All the state institutions established west of the Alleghenies before 1830 were begun under Presbyterian direction.[2]

For the first two decades of the nineteenth century, Methodists and Baptists accepted more or less as a matter of course the Presbyterian and Congregational control of higher education throughout the country, but particularly in the West. But beginning in the eighteen-twenties and continuing until the Civil War, the Methodists and Baptists entered upon a period of college founding unprecedented in the history of denominational activity. In 1830 the Methodists had not established a single permanent college; from 1830 to the Civil War they had planted thirty-four permanent colleges. By 1830 the Baptists had already established four colleges; in 1861 there were twenty-five Baptist colleges in the country. From 1837 to 1855 the Disciples established five colleges; during the same period the Quakers founded two colleges, and the United Brethren one. Of the colleges founded west of the Allegheny Mountains during the first half of the last century an overwhelming majority were established and fostered

---

[2] Gewehr, *op. cit.*, chapter ix, "The Founding of Colleges," 219–234.

by the revivalistic Churches, and in all of them revivalism was kept continuously alive. Oberlin College furnishes an interesting example of the revivalistic influence in American college education. Its most famous president, Charles G. Finney (1851–1866), was, as we have seen, one of the greatest of American revivalistic preachers of all time, and under his leadership Oberlin became one of the most important revival centers in the country.[3] That American higher education should be democratic rather than aristocratic was largely a contribution of the revivalistic Churches. It was their multiplication of colleges over the land that was more responsible than anything else for the decentralizing of educational facilities, that determined that higher education should not be confined to a few colleges located in distant centers, and that educational opportunity should be fully decentralized and available for all.[4] Speaking before the *Society for the Promotion of Collegiate and Theological Education in the West* in 1851 Absalom Peters, the Secretary of the American Home Missionary Society, thus explains the democratization of higher education:

The wide extent of country, the prospective increase of population, the form of government, the independence of the states,

---

[3] D. G. Tewksbury, *The Founding of American Colleges and Universities before the Civil War with particular reference to the Religious Influences bearing upon the College Movement* (New York, 1932).

[4] See W. W. Sweet, *Indiana Asbury-DePauw University, 1837–1937: A Hundred Years of Higher Education in the Middle West* (New York, 1937), chapter i. Also P. G. Mode, *The Frontier Spirit in American Christianity* (New York, 1923), chapter iv, "The Small College," 59–78.

and above all, the Protestant principle of universal education have forbidden such a design (the planting of a few colleges at great distances from each other); and the colleges have adapted themselves to their appropriate spheres, in accordance with this state of things. They have thus trained the public mind to feel that a college, in each district of convenient extent, is a blessing to the people. It is therefore placed beyond all doubt that in our country, in the whole extent of it, it is to be a land of colleges.[5]

Lyman Beecher, one of the principal promoters of revivalism of the Congregational-Presbyterian kind, in his time, utters these ringing words for education in his *Plea for the West*: [6]

We must educate! We must educate! or we must perish by our own prosperity. If we do not, short from the cradle to the grave will be our race. If, in our haste to be rich and mighty, we outrun our literary and religious institutions, they will never overtake us; or only come up after the battle of liberty is fought and lost, as spoils to grace the victory, and as resources of inexorable despotism for the perpetuity of our bondage. Let no man at the East quiet himself, and dream of liberty, whatever may become of the West. Our alliance of blood, and political institutions, and common interests, is such that we cannot stand aloof in the hour of her calamity, should it ever come. Her destiny is our destiny; and the day that her gallant ship goes down, our little boat sinks in the vortex.

---

[5] Absalom Peters, *Discourse Before the Society for the Promotion of Collegiate and Theological Education in the West* (pamphlet) (1851), 13.
[6] Cincinnati, 1835, 270.

III

The many reform movements which swept over the English-speaking world in the latter eighteenth and early nineteenth centuries owed much of their impetus to revivalism. The new humanitarian impulse which lay back of all such movements has a direct relationship to the revivalistic emphasis upon the inestimable worth of each individual soul. If all men are equal in God's sight then it behooves Christian men to see to it that the underprivileged, the unfortunate, and the downtrodden have a better chance in this world.

The men back of the crusade in England to abolish the slave trade—William Wilberforce, Granville Sharp, and Thomas Clarkson—were evangelicals. Up to about the middle of the eighteenth century, slavery and the slave trade had been accepted as a matter of course. Although slavery had been outlawed in England (by Lord Mansfield's decision in 1792 that any slave brought to England automatically became free), many Englishmen had grown rich through the slave trade. It has been estimated that the English slave traders alone, from first to last, shipped something like two million Negroes to America. One of the results of the eighteenth-century revivals was the tendering of men's consciences in regard to such matters as the slave trade and the holding of human beings in bondage. As the evangelical movement grew in England, the number of slavery haters likewise increased. They were joined by men like William Pitt, Edmund Burke, and Charles James Fox

—men imbued with the revolutionary philosophy that all men are created equal and have the right to life, liberty, and the pursuit of happiness. Together these two groups were eventually able in 1807 to force through Parliament the bill fathered by Wilberforce to abolish the slave trade. In this connection it is of interest to recall that the last known letter that John Wesley ever wrote was to William Wilberforce and it deserves quoting. The letter is dated February 24, 1791 (he died on March 2):

Dear Sir:

Unless the divine power has raised you up to be as *Athanasius contra mundum,* I see not how you can go through your glorious enterprise in opposing that execrable villany, which is the scandal of religion, of England, and of human nature. Unless God has raised you up for this very thing, you will be worn out by the opposition of men and devils. But if God be for you, who can be against you? Are all men together stronger than God? O be not weary in well doing! Go on, in the name of God and in the power of his might, till even American slavery (the vilest that ever saw the sun) shall vanish away before it. . . .

That He who has guided you from youth up may continue to strengthen you in this and all things is the prayer of, dear sir,

Your affectionate servant,

John Wesley.

That Wilberforce was in full accord with the religious implications expressed by Wesley is shown by the follow-

ing sentence from a letter he wrote before the abolition
debate in the Commons in 1791:

May I look to Him for wisdom and strength and the power
of persuasion. And ascribe to Him all the praise if I succeed;
and if I fail, say from the heart, "Thy will be done." [1]

The story of the relationship of the evangelical groups
to slavery in Virginia has been excellently told by Professor
Gewehr in his *Great Awakening in Virginia* (chapter x).
All the revivalistic religious bodies in the southern colonies
developed strong anti-slavery views and, by the close of the
War for Independence, manumission of slaves had become
increasingly common, particularly among those people who
had been religiously awakened. The revival had also
reached great numbers of Negroes and many slaves were
received into the Church. The Presbyterians, Baptists, and
Methodists took strong official anti-slavery action in the
seventeen-eighties.

The first anti-slavery impulse in New England came
from Samuel Hopkins, the minister of First Congregational Church in Newport, Rhode Island, one of the most
active slave-trading ports in America. Hopkins was the
principal exponent of the revivalistic Calvinism of Jonathan Edwards, stressing particularly the Doctrine of Disinterested Benevolence—the idea that holiness consists in
disinterested benevolence or disinterested love for "being
in general." Since Negroes, Indians, and underprivileged

---

[1] See *The Letters of the Rev. John Wesley*, 8 vols. Edited by John Telford (London, 1931), VIII, 264–265. See also Wesley's letter to Granville
Sharp, October 11, 1787 (*ibid.*, 16–17). Sharp had taken a leading part in
the organization of the *Society for the Abolition of Slavery* in 1787.

people, wherever they may be, are a part of "being in general," they must come in for their just share of the true Christian's concern. It was this emphasis in New England theology that was largely responsible for the reinvigorating of New England religious life, and for the sending out of an ever-increasing stream of young men imbued with these ideas, who were to take the leadership in many of the reform movements in America during the first half of the last century. Young men went about asking themselves "Am I willing to be damned for the glory of God?" [2] A part of Samuel Hopkins' theological system was a general atonement—that is, that Christ died to save *all* sinners, Indians and Negroes, as well as New England Congregationalists.

Early nineteenth-century revivalism, likewise, was the creator of strong anti-slavery sentiment. David Rice, the father of Presbyterianism in Kentucky, held that the slave was as much a creature of God and as entitled to his liberty as was his master, and that slavery was entirely out of harmony with the republican form of government. Many of the frontier Baptist preachers were strong advocates of emancipation of the slaves. David Barrow, a well-known Virginia Baptist preacher, was convinced that slavery was contrary to the laws of God and nature as well as inconsistent with republican forms of government and, in order to escape from it, he moved over the mountains. Recently I have discovered letters from numerous Virginia Methodists who moved to Ohio in the early eighteen hundreds in order to get away from the iniquitous institution. Their

---

[2] See *The Works of Samuel Hopkins*, etc., 3 vols. (Boston, 1854), I, chapter xii, Section iv, "Disinterested Affection," 378–399.

letters to Virginia relatives contain numerous references to the satisfaction they feel in living in a land of liberty, and they are constantly urging their Virginia relatives to join them. One slave-holding Methodist bemoans his owner-ship of slaves, stating that:

. . . they are a hell to us in this world, and I fear will be so in the next. But what to do with them, I know not. We cannot live with them or without them; and what to do is a question . . . unless the whip is forever on their backs, they do noth-ing. . . . Is this a life for a Christian to lead? I wish some good advice upon this head.[3]

Among the most interesting anti-slavery movements in the early years of the last century was that among western Baptists. In 1807 the anti-slavery Baptists in Kentucky organized a separate Association of anti-slavery Baptist Churches which was known as the "Friends of Humanity Association." It adopted what was known as Tarrant's Rules, the first one being that no person was to be admitted to the churches composing the Association if he appeared friendly to perpetual slavery. Another rule provided that in no case was a member to purchase a slave except to rescue a slave from perpetual slavery, and even in such a case it was to be done in such a way as the churches ap-proved. "Friends of Humanity Associations" were later formed in Illinois and Missouri, all pledged to the same anti-slavery principles.[4]

---

[3] *The Dromgoole Papers* (MSS. in the University of North Carolina; microfilms at the University of Chicago).

[4] W. W. Sweet, *Religion on the American Frontier: The Baptists* (New York, 1931), chapter v, "Anti-Slavery Movements among Baptists," 77–101.

The abolition movement fathered by William Lloyd Garrison found its largest support in New England among Baptists and Methodists, and not among Congregationalists and Unitarians as has been generally assumed. Too much credit, or discredit, for the abolition movement has been given to conspicuous Unitarian leaders such as Theodore Parker, whereas it would have amounted to little if there had not been a large following in the rural towns and countryside where the revivalistic churches had their greatest strength.[5]

The most startling connection between revivalism and the anti-slavery movement was that which centered at Lane Theological Seminary in Cincinnati, and later transferred to Oberlin College. The outstanding figure in this phase of the movement was Theodore Dwight Weld, one of Charles G. Finney's converts and one of his most ardent followers. Weld, a man of remarkable personality and of extraordinary ability, entered Lane Theological Seminary as a student at its opening in 1832. He had promised Lewis Tappan, a philanthropic New York businessman who had given Lane its first endowment, to agitate and discuss among the students the abolition of slavery. So successful was he in his endeavor that within a few months practically the entire student body were converted to the cause, even some of the southern students. Not content merely

[5] G. H. Barnes, *The Anti-Slavery Impulse* (New York, 1933), 90–91. See also in Notes, 242. A check on the delegates attending the Anti-Slavery Society convention in 1835 showed that two-thirds were ministers, and two-thirds of them were either Baptists or Methodists. It was assumed by Bostonians that Boston was the moral reform center of the nation, which is certainly not borne out as far as anti-slavery reform is concerned. In this respect Boston lagged far behind the rural and small town. *Ibid.*, 91, 242.

to accept the abolition of slavery as a theory, the students began to work at it and set out to elevate the blacks in and about Cincinnati. They opened schools, reading rooms, and libraries for them; and there was much mingling of Lane students with the colored population of Cincinnati. This, of course, aroused bitter opposition in certain quarters in Cincinnati and ugly rumors were afloat that social amalgamation between Negroes and Lane students was actually under way. At this juncture the Lane trustees, resident in Cincinnati—President Lyman Beecher was at the time in the East—stepped in and attempted to handle the situation. The student abolition society was abolished and the students were forbidden to discuss the subject. This was the signal for a student revolt, and by the time President Beecher had returned the rebel students had withdrawn from the Seminary and had rented a house in the city where Asa Mahan, the one professor who agreed with the students, was conducting classes. Eventually the majority of the Lane rebels were persuaded to migrate to Oberlin, then just in its infancy, and Asa Mahan became the first President. The students had agreed to go to Oberlin only on the condition that Charles G. Finney should be brought to Oberlin as professor of theology.[6] This was accordingly done, and Finney continued to carry on both as a revivalist and a teacher. His solution of the slavery issue was to con-

---

[6] This dramatic story is well told in Barnes, *op. cit.*, chapters vi, "The Lane Debate," and vii, "The Lane Rebels," and viii, "The Weld Agency." See also the *Autobiography and Correspondence of Lyman Beecher*, 2 vols. (New York, 1865), II, 321, 326, 345. See also Fletcher, *op. cit.*, I, chapter xviii, "Hotbed of Abolitionism."

vert the slaveholders and all his early students, who went forth from Oberlin to carry on anti-slavery evangelism, used the Finney methods. It was this movement which created a new anti-slavery impulse destined to be far more important historically than Garrisonian abolition.

IV

That period in American history from about 1830 to 1860 has been most aptly termed "The Sentimental Years." [1] It was a period in which organized benevolence flourished in a hitherto unheard-of fashion. Missionary societies, home and foreign, for the conversion of the heathen, came into existence in bewildering numbers. Bible and Tract Societies were organized with the slogan "Put a Bible in every home and a tract in every hand." Societies were formed to advance the cause of temperance; to promote Sunday Schools; to save sailors at the ports and along the canals; to fight the use of tobacco; to improve the diet; to advance the cause of peace; to reform prisons; to stop prostitution; to colonize Negroes in Africa; to support education. There was scarcely an object of benevolence for the advancement of which some institution had not been formed.[2] The greatest among these organizations had no formal connection with the churches, outside missionary societies, but they were all the legitimate children of the revivalism of the time. There were eight great

---

[1] E. Douglas Branch, *The Sentimental Years, 1836–1860* (New York, 1934).
[2] Barnes, *op. cit.*, chapter ii, "The New York Philanthropists," 18–28.

societies—"The Great Eight" as they were called—which were largely officered by New School Presbyterian revivalistic laymen, most of whom had come under the influence of Charles G. Finney. The most conspicuous of these were the brothers, Lewis and Arthur Tappan, wealthy New York merchants whose benevolent giving reached out in every direction and took in every good cause.

It has been stated that wherever Charles G. Finney went he always left behind scores of young men "emancipated from sin and Calvinism and overflowing with benevolence for unsaved mankind." The gospel he preached encouraged men to "work as well as believe," and as a result there was always a "mighty influence toward reform." Perhaps the chief significance of Charles G. Finney lies not so much in the fact that he was the instrument in adding tens of thousands to the active ranks of the American churches, as in the circumstance that these new converts became active participants in every forward movement of their time.

Gilbert Seldes, in his *Stammering Century*,[3] makes the statement that the revivals of the 1820's and '30's were the last to have any profound effect upon the social and intellectual life of the American people. He states that the revival of 1857, which followed a great financial panic, was not constructive socially. This statement is evidently based on a too-limited knowledge of the facts. For out of that revival came the introduction of the Y.M.C.A. into American cities. It produced the leadership, such as that of

---

[3] (New York, 1928), 141.

Dwight L. Moody, out of which came the religious work carried on in the armies during the Civil War. It gave impetus to the creation of the Christian and Sanitary Commissions, and to the numerous Freedmen's Societies which were formed in the midst of the War. It is a significant fact that all benevolent enterprises flourished during the Civil War, and the period saw charities on a larger scale than ever before.[4] Though war always loosens the purse strings, charitable giving at any time must depend chiefly upon people whose sympathies are the most touched by the sufferings of their fellowmen, and in the great majority of instances they are the ones whose hearts have been warmed by a divine flame.

---

[4] Emerson David Fite, *Social and Industrial Conditions in the North during the Civil War* (New York, 1910), especially chapter xi, "Charity."

CHAPTER EIGHT

REVIVALISM ON THE WANE

VOLUME EIGHT of the *History of American Life*, covering
the years 1865 to 1878, is entitled *The Emergence of
Modern America*.[1] That title implies that the years under
consideration were a period of transition; that America
after the Civil War was a very different America than that
which saw the opening of the great struggle for the pres-
ervation of the Union. The country was no longer pre-
dominately a frontier and although new populations from
Europe were moving rapidly into the great prairie regions
they were brought to their new homes by steamboat and
rail, and the day of the oxcart and the covered wagon was
rapidly fading into the past.

The ninth volume in the *History of American Life* is
called the *Rise of the City, 1878–1898*. This likewise implies a rapid change in the economic and social climate of
America. Some of you may have heard Bishop F. J. McConnell's apt illustration of the influence of climatic change.
When he was a boy he was fascinated by a book in his
father's library full of pictures of the age of the Dinosauria
and the Dinotherium, the monstrous reptiles and immense
mammals of the elephant family, and the saber-tooth tigers
which roamed the earth before it became a human habita-

---

[1] By Allan Nevins (New York, 1927). Vol. IX, A. M. Schlesinger, *The
Rise of the City, 1878–1898* (New York, 1933).

tion. He was puzzled to know how it was possible to rid the earth of these monsters and what became of them. But when he grew to young manhood, went to college, and began to study the science of the earth he learned that it was all very simple; there was a change of climate and they all eventually died off. Of course, not all at once, but as the ages passed they gradually disappeared. Exactly the same law applies to social and religious institutions. As the social, cultural, and religious climate in America changed, the social, cultural, and religious institutions gradually changed likewise. The purpose in this last chapter is to trace the changes which have taken place in American revivalism largely as a result of the changes in the cultural, economic, social, and religious climate.

I

The years following the War between the States saw rapid cultural changes in the two principal revivalistic Churches, the Methodists and the Baptists. At the beginning of the nineteenth century, the educational and cultural chasm between the Churches which had a college-trained ministry and those in which the educational standards for the ministry were practically non-existent was deep and wide. The end of the century saw that gulf considerably lessened. Clerical culture and learning were no longer a monopoly of the Congregationalists, the Presbyterians, and the Episcopalians. Education, refinement, and dignity now characterized the ministry and services of many Methodists, the Baptists, and the Disciples, equally with those of the formerly élite churches. Indeed the Methodists in the towns and cities by the end of the century began to get out the robes and prayer books which had been carefully put aside in the early years of the Church's independent existence, and many of them in form and ritual went far beyond Presbyterianism and Congregationalism.

There was a corresponding change also in the cultural and educational status of the laity of the revivalistic Churches. The denominational colleges following the Civil War grew with amazing rapidity, and the Methodist and Baptist institutions outnumbered all others. The result was the mounting numbers of college graduates sitting in Baptist, Methodist, and Disciples' pews. This does not mean necessarily that revivalism and education were mutually exclusive, but it did mean that an excessive emotional appeal would no longer be effective. Without doubt, the presence of an educated and cool-headed leadership exercises a restraining influence on an overemotionalized company of people. Deep feeling may spread with the utmost abandon through a congregation under a vivid emotional appeal unless there are a number of controlled individuals present—people accustomed to subordinate feeling to rational considerations. These will act as bulwarks against the advancing tide of emotionalism; where there are educated persons in any congregation and an educated minister in the pulpit, there is small chance that an extreme emotional revivalism will arise. On the other hand, a congregation made up of people with little education or critical training may easily be led into emotional excess by a revivalistic preacher, who gives way to his own deep feeling, who shouts and gesticulates wildly, while tears stream down his face as he speaks. Highly emotionalized revivalism has always made the greatest appeal to persons of little education. The emotions of such persons "pass swiftly and impulsively into action." [1] In pioneer communities, where the emphasis was placed upon bodily development at the expense of mental equipment and where there were no people of educational attainment, revivalism of the extreme emotional type naturally flourished. It was the changing cultural climate that has been responsible for the elimination of much of the extravagant type of revivalism.

The great number of old Methodist camp meeting grounds to be found all over the United States, still owned by the Conferences or camp meeting associations but now turned into middle-class summer resorts or meeting places for summer conferences, are mute witnesses to the social, religious, and cultural change which has taken place in American Methodism. The conditions which gave rise to the camp meeting have passed. With the construction of larger and more adequate church buildings, and the introduction of the protracted meeting type of revivalism held during the winter months, the need for the great summer gatherings in the woods, as harvest time for souls, gradu-

---

[1] F. M. Davenport in his *Primitive Traits in Religious Revivals,* chapter i, advanced three laws which help explain emotional revivalism from the psychological standpoint. These are the law of *sympathetic likemindedness,* the law of *spread,* and the law of *restraint.* See also Elizabeth K. Nottingham, *Methodism and the Frontier, Indiana Proving Ground* (New York, 1941), chapter ix, "Revivalism in England and America."

ally disappeared. During the seventies and eighties, and on to the end of the century, what were called camp meetings continued to be held but their nature underwent swift change. At Chautauqua, New York, the old camp meeting ground was transformed (1874) under the leadership of John H. Vincent, later a bishop of the Methodist Church, into an institution whose influence spread all over the nation.

Starting as a movement to increase the effectiveness of Sunday School instruction, with courses on Sunday School management and Bible teaching, it expanded within a few years into a veritable university. In 1878 home-study courses in literary and scientific subjects were introduced. The following years courses were offered for secular school teachers, and in rapid succession Schools of Science and Mathematics, Library Training, Domestic Science, Music, Arts and Crafts, Physical Education, and, in co-operation with Cornell University, a School of Agriculture (1912) were formed. Large lecture halls, a theatre, club houses, a library, and a gymnasium were erected; and between 1924 and 1932 forty-five thousand people attended the general assembly each year, where they heard famous preachers and lecturers, attended concerts, and in other ways absorbed culture.[2]

By the end of the century little Chautauquas had sprung up all over the country and many of them were utilizing old camp meeting grounds. It was a poor town indeed that did not have at least a week of lectures and

---

[2] J. L. Hurlburt, *The Story of Chautauqua.*

entertainment some time during the summer months. After 1900 the traveling Chautauquas appeared and companies were formed to supply talent, while college boys were utilized as advance agents to sell the courses to the communities and later to put up the tents and perform the other necessary menial tasks. Such has been the strange development of the camp meeting, a by-product which the old camp meeting preachers would doubtless have hotly repudiated, but a transformation which was inevitable in the light of the change in the cultural and religious climate.

II

The astonishing growth of American cities from 1880 to the end of the century was one of the marvels of the age. This growth was due to the attractive power of manufacturing centers, drawing population from the small towns and rural communities, and to an even greater degree from the overcrowded countries of Europe. Between 1880 and 1890 the rural population declined not only in the old New England states, but in such states as Ohio, Indiana, Illinois, and Iowa. During the last two decades of the nineteenth century, the foreign-born population of the great cities reached such proportions as to cause grave apprehension that the basic American ideals and principles would be completely swamped by the great mass of the foreign-born. From the close of the Civil War to 1900, no less than 13,260,000 foreigners of all kinds entered the United States, more than double the population of New England. Following the turn of the century the number entering this country was even larger. In the year 1889, sixty-eight of the towns of Massachusetts, including the largest, were governed by the Irish. The flocking of these newcomers to the cities, both native-born as well as the foreign-born, created problems of all sorts, not alone affecting politics and social conditions but also religion. Thus again a religious crisis was created through mass immigration, comparable to that of the early part of the last century as a result of the western movement of population. Again great masses of people were cutting themselves loose from their old homes, their churches, their schools, and their old neighbors to find new homes in the rapidly developing American cities. In the cities religion had to meet a type of competition which it had never before experienced, in the cafes, beer-gardens, shooting galleries, amusement parks, saloons, theatres, and, in more recent times, moving pictures, night clubs, prize fights, professional baseball, and a host of other types of entertainment.[1] In the light of the kind of competition it had to meet, it becomes clear how and why a new type of spectacular city revivalism arose.

It was the city which gave rise to the professional revivalist. There had been a few men, such as Asahel Nettleton, in the early part of the nineteenth century who devoted all their time to revivalism, but the vocational evangelist came into existence with the rise of the city.

---

[1] A. M. Schlesinger, *Political and Social Growth of the United States, 1852–1933* (New York, 1933), 226, 281–282. See also A. M. Schlesinger, *Rise of the City.*

The greatest of all the professional revivalists was undoubtedly Dwight L. Moody. His evangelistic career began immediately following the Civil War, and ended with his death in the very midst of a great meeting in Kansas City in 1899. All his great meetings were city campaigns conducted in Brooklyn, Philadelphia, New York, Chicago, Boston, St. Louis, San Francisco. Conservative in theology, a literalist in his interpretation of Scripture though never a bigot, with a flat voice, often ungrammatical in speech, with sermons preached over and over again, Moody's success in pointing men to the Christian way of life was truly astonishing. In 1875, on his return from his first great evangelistic campaign in England, he said to a friend: "I am the most overestimated man in this country. By some means the people look upon me as a great man, but I am only a lay preacher and have little learning." One newspaper reporter, covering his meetings in a certain city, stated that there was never a moment when he was eloquent; that he cared not a whit for logic; that he murdered the English language; that he had never seen the inside of a geology; and yet he stated there was not another man in America that could have filled the vast auditorium day after day. He held, during these meetings, forty-eight thousand people in the hollow of his hand, and they wept and smiled as he willed.[2] The attempts of sociologists and the psychologists to explain him seem trite and foolish. Some have suggested

[2] Gamaliel Bradford, *Dwight L. Moody, A Worker in Souls* (New York, 1927). See also W. W. Sweet, *The Makers of Christianity from John Cotton to Lyman Abbott* (New York, 1937), 266–278.

that his "unusual earnestness and simplicity" were the things that kept his hearers enchained. The impression he left was that there was truth behind the man greater than he. But whatever the explanation, the fact cannot be gainsaid that he was a wonderfully effective human instrument through which Divine grace was mediated to men.

The city evangels who followed Moody—Reuben Torrey, Wilbur Chapman, B. Fay Mills, Sam Jones, George Stuart, W. E. Biederwolf, and Billy Sunday—were all more or less in the Moody tradition, though none ever equaled him in the total and lasting influence which they exerted. They, too, were all conservative in their theology, the majority of them being Presbyterians. Some of them, as Reuben Torrcy, were college graduates; others, as Billy Sunday, were without formal schooling. All preached a simple, easily-understood gospel message. Some of them were dramatic in their preaching, and all were assisted by evangelistic singers who not only performed themselves but organized great choirs made up of local talent for the period of the meeting. In the latter years of this type of city evangelism, there was great emphasis placed on highly organized machinery set up by business agents, who demanded that great sums of money be subscribed before the meetings could begin. "Billy" Sunday carried the "Big time" evangelism to an extreme equaled by none of his contemporaries. He utilized almost to perfection the techniques of big business in organizing his campaigns and very large sums of money were subscribed to carry them forward. He claims to have preached to eighty millions of people during the course of his career.

He always rated large headlines in the newspapers and in other ways attracted the attention of the public generally. This technique, however, by the middle of the nineteen-twenties had begun to pall on the public and during the last years of his life his influence and popularity had greatly declined.

We are too near the era of the vocational evangelists to appraise correctly their contribution. They undoubtedly rendered a type of service in our large cities which perhaps could not have been performed by any other agency. They reached thousands of people who had lost contact with the churches; they fought the grosser sins common to city life and they lifted moral standards. None seems to have effected any large social reform, except as that was brought about through reformed lives. Billy Sunday, however, did have a determining influence in bringing in the dry era.

Growing more or less directly out of the Moody influence was a new type of college and university revivalism, very different from the older type which had followed the usual patterns. This new college revivalism, carried on through the medium of college Y.M.- and Y.W.C.A.'s centered in an appeal for the dedication of young life to the cause of converting the world in a generation. Thus religion, with a definite and challenging task to perform, was brought to hundreds of college campuses through the medium of such dynamic leaders as John R. Mott, Robert E. Speer, and Sherwood Eddy. As a result of their labors and influence, literally thousands of students went out from the colleges and universities of the land as crusaders for the cause of bringing in the reign of Christ throughout the world. Student Volunteer Bands were formed in the colleges constituting living centers of religious influence.[3]

During the very years when Moody revivalism was at its height, the Salvation Army was introduced from England to America. It made its appearance here just two years after its establishment in England (1878). In ten years it had marched across the continent and was carrying on its work in every large city in America. Using the old revivalistic methods, with preaching based upon the reality of sin, the divinity of Christ, and his atoning death, and the awful reality of hell, its primary concern has always been and still is to reach and convert people who have met defeat in the struggle of life. They believe that the love of God is as wide as the world; the atoning sacrifice is as universal as human need. Combined with their revivalism they carried on a tremendous work in social service. In 1936 there were 1,088 corps; 103,038 officers and soldiers; and nearly forty millions of property. It conducts workingmen's hotels, food depots, industrial homes, farm colonies, second-hand stores, children's homes, employment bureaus, day nurseries, slum settlements, distributes free ice and coal among the poor, gives outings to mothers and children. In short, it fully lives up to its "Articles of War" which pledges every soldier to fight unendingly against all sin and sinful conditions in our cities.[4]

---

[3] William M. Beahm, "Factors in the Development of the Student Volunteer Movement for Foreign Missions" (Typed Ph.D. thesis, University of Chicago, 1941).

[4] Of the 1,088 Salvation Army churches, 1,067 are urban (Census of 1936).

Occupying a position at the opposite pole from the Salvation Army is the Oxford Group Movement, fathered by an American Lutheran, Frank Buchman. This is a type of revivalism which has appealed especially to large numbers of students in universities and colleges, and to persons in the upper economic and cultural levels. It is a very personal type of approach, and its early converts were won by personal talks with students at Oxford and Cambridge. Its principal emphasis is upon the guidance that God can and will furnish for every individual; it teaches that God has a plan for every life, but when through personal sin that plan is spoiled "God is always ready with another." To lead the kind of life God has planned for us a person must be willing to surrender "will, time, possessions, family, ambitions." Theologically, Buchmanism is entirely orthodox; it has been characterized as "orthodoxy galvanized into new life in modern conditions." The movement has had its largest success among the so-called upper classes, where sex and money have been primarily responsible for wrecking God's plan for lives. It is an interesting fact that in America the influence of Buchmanism has been primarily exerted among Episcopalians. It has been suggested that just as the Salvation Army was formed to deal with the "downs and outs," the Buchman movement is primarily concerned, and has had its largest success, with the "ups and outs."

Still another type of city revivalism is that which has been carried on by revivalistic cults such as the International Church of the Four Square Gospel. It was founded by Aimée Semple McPherson, an unusual woman who began her career as an evangelist at seventeen years of age and after extensive evangelistic work in the United States, Canada, England, and Australia, came to Los Angeles in 1918. Here her star rose rapidly and in 1921 she had gained a sufficient following to erect a great auditorium seating five thousand (dedicated, 1923) called the "Angelus Temple Church of the Four Square Gospel." She acquired the ownership of a radio station and established a Bible College called the "Lighthouse of International Four Square Evangelism," where Four Square Gospel ministers receive their training. The Angelus Temple with the Bible College constitute a most effective organization for the carrying on of the old type of revivalism with all the showmanship of the most modern kind. For membership, evidence of "born again experience" is required. In 1936 two hundred and five branch organizations were reported throughout the country with a total membership of some sixteen thousand, of which more than eighty per cent are found in cities.[5]

III

The waning of revivalism in most of the large evangelical bodies has been one of the principal factors in creating numerous new revivalistic sects. These have arisen in large numbers since 1880. Most of them were established on a

---

[5] *Religious Bodies*, 1936 (Washington: United States Department of Commerce, Bureau of the Census, 1941), Vol. II, Part I, 739–746. Of the 205 churches reported in 1936, all but 54 were urban.

continuous revivalistic basis and are generally relatively small. The Southern Baptist Convention, however, is a striking exception. The largest of all the Baptist bodies in the United States, it reported in 1937 four and a half million members. Its continued emphasis upon the old type of revivalism is to a large part explained by the fact that of the 13,815 churches reported in 1936, 11,972 were rural churches, while less than two thousand were to be found in urban centers. Among the largest of the revivalistic sects, including the Assemblies of God, the Church of God (Anderson, Indiana), Church of Christ, Conservative Dunkers, Progressive Dunkers, Pentecostal Holiness, Pentecostal Assemblies of Jesus Christ, and Pilgrim Holiness, which were reported in 1936, there were 12,091 congregations and of this number 7,630 were rural.[1]

Some of the new revivalistic bodies, as the Nazarene, have succeeded well both in rural and urban environments, and are about equally divided between city and country communities. They appeal, however, as do all the others, to people belonging to about the same cultural and economic level. Perhaps it is not out of place to class all of these bodies as Churches of the disinherited; or Churches of the underprivileged. Among them the old type of revivalism succeeds and they reach large numbers of people who do not feel at home in the larger evangelical Churches. During the period of the depression they constituted prob-

---

[1] See M. E. Gaddis, *Perfectionism in America*. (Typed Ph.D. thesis, University of Chicago, 1929.) Also see Elmer T. Clark, *The Small Sects in America* (Nashville, 1937).

ably the most rapidly growing religious bodies in the United States. For instance, the Assemblies of God, formed in 1914, had, in 1926, 48,000 members; in 1937 they reported 175,000 and 3,470 churches. The Church of God with headquarters in Cleveland, Tennessee, increased in ten years, 1926 to 1937, about four hundred per cent. Similar revivalistic bodies have also risen among the Negroes in the cities as well as in the rural sections of the South. Besides the usual revivalistic doctrines, all of these bodies stress premillennialism and the doctrine of holiness. Their God is a God of love, who cares for their condition, and with whom they can walk and talk. This close relationship with God is obtained through a conversion experience, which is often accompanied with joyful acclaim. The members of these Churches stress puritan virtues, together with total abstinence from all harmful habits. The very fact they have increased so rapidly is an indication that they occupy a necessary place among the religious organizations of our day, and are supplying needs and reaching people which at present seem to be beyond the power of the "enlightened" Churches to supply or reach.

In spite of the fine work which has been done these past forty years to achieve a larger Church unity in America, there seems to me to be no likelihood that there will be secured any great degree of unity in our time.[2] What Church unions will be achieved will be among the upper-middle-class Churches, since they have been growing more

[2] W. W. Sweet, "Rapprochement in American Protestantism" (*Religion in Life*, Vol. XI, Winter Number, 1941–42, 74–83).

and more alike and have been finding more and more ways in which they can cooperate. But while this is going on, new submerged groups will continue to form on the fringes, some of which will grow numerically strong and eventually emerge as middle-class Churches, gradually changing their methods and emphasis. As long as American society is made up of such uneven social, economic, and cultural groups, such diversity of religion will of necessity continue. This fact we must recognize, even if we can do very little to remedy it in the face of the present organization of society. A practice very common among the "respectable Churches" is to denounce these underprivileged groups; to call them all "Holy Rollers"; to sneer at them as trouble-makers. I have heard ministers say that they were glad that such groups existed, for into them trouble-makers in their own Churches were drained off. It is well to bear in mind that Baptists, Methodists, Disciples, and Quakers were once trouble-makers for the respectable Churches—the Congregationalists, the Presbyterians, and the Episcopalians. And only a little farther back in time, the Episcopalians, the Congregationalists, and the Presbyterians were, in their turn, trouble-makers. As some one has suggested, it is "the cranks" which turn the world.

IV

The Churches which have the largest membership today are those bodies which in the past have profited most from revivalism, a type of religion that is dominantly personal. Revivalism tends to disappear when the impersonal becomes dominant over the personal. Charles Sumner once remarked to Julia Ward Howe, the author of the "Battle Hymn of the Republic," that he no longer was interested in individuals, but only in causes. To that remark Julia Ward Howe replied, "God Almighty has not gone that far, yet." It would seem that in a democracy the personal emphasis in religion would naturally find its largest development. And so it has been, and it would seem that it should remain so. The emphasis in our American democracy upon the freedom of conscience gives personal religion its opportunity, and the great evangelical Churches are living witnesses to what extent that opportunity has been appropriated. One of the principal reasons why revivalism is on the wane among all the larger evangelical Churches is because of strong impersonalizing trends that have been in process for more than a generation.

In the last fifty years the great American Churches and their leaders, like Charles Sumner, have grown less and less interested in individuals and more and more concerned with the advancement of causes. No doubt what we call the Social Gospel emphasis has been partly responsible for this growing trend. Gaius Glenn Atkins has remarked that the Social Gospel saved the Protestant pulpit, meaning that it gave preachers live subjects to treat in their pulpits, when the old-time subjects, due to liberal trends in theology, seemed to be outworn. But, at the same time, it undermined the personal in religion. Social and economic justice became the principal theme of all the Social Gospel preachers: the Harry Emerson Fosdicks, the Ernest F.

Tittles, the Albert E. Days, the Charles C. Morrisons, and others of their kind, and all the lesser Social Gospel preachers followed in their train. When I was a student in the seminary, we were going to save the world by becoming proficient in sociology and many of us rushed over to Columbia University to take graduate courses in sociology under Giddings. The Social Gospel advocates insisted that you cannot make a better world by "snatching brands from the burning," by proceeding with the conversion of people one by one. They insisted that the Church must deal with society as a whole, with basic causes for sinful living. In their enthusiasm to save society they overlooked sinners. Revivalism, they held, was ineffective, out of date, and must therefore be discarded. It may have served a good purpose in the past, but its usefulness was gone.

Then came the first World War furnishing other great impersonal themes for the pulpit, such as the saving of democracy. Then came the Treaty of Versailles and the peace crusade which followed its tragic failure. The peace theme furnished the greatest preachers in the land with sermon subjects for a decade and more. If they were not preaching world peace, they were occupied with race discrimination; bettering international relations; promoting better race relations; furthering international justice. All interesting subjects and many great sermons were built around them, but under such preaching few in the pews ever felt singled out. Many who sat under such preaching no doubt were in full agreement with the preacher and agreed that something ought to be done about it, but as far

as they themselves were concerned there was little urge
for them to be better men and women. They felt no personal responsibility in the matter, and nothing particularly
happened. A few economic royalists got mad and stormed
out of the church, leaving their pews vacant; others
changed their membership to churches whose ministers
preached the "old-fashioned" gospel where they could be
at ease in Zion.

Added to this has been the growing influence of religious education, stressing the Horace Bushnell emphasis
upon Christian nurture. Thus religion came to be, especially in the large town and city churches, more and more
a matter of learning and less and less a matter of feeling.
Religious educators have said a great deal about making religion pupil-centered rather than content-centered, with the
unhappy result that in their attempt to make religious instruction fit the everyday need of the child they overlooked
the long religious experience of mankind. Here too the emphasis has been upon the person's relationship to society,
rather than his relationship to God; upon the evils of
society rather than upon personal selfishness. In its re-
action against the old revivalism, with its overemphasis
upon the emotional and the personal, the Church has
tended to establish an impersonal and institutional pattern
of salvation almost as rigid as that represented by the state
Churches of Europe in the seventeenth and eighteenth
centuries.

It would be unfortunate if not fatal to religion in a
democracy to think of it entirely in terms of society or of

an institution. The basic doctrine in democracy is the emphasis upon individual worth. Likewise one of the basic doctrines of evangelical Christianity is the infinite value which God places upon each individual. Perhaps it is inevitable, and fortunately so, that never again can religion be as exclusively personal as it was in the heyday of American revivalism. The day of rugged individualism is past. In the realm of business as well as in the realm of religion, it is necessary to think more and more in terms of society. But the American way of life would be lost entirely if individualism were completely destroyed.

The suspicion under which emotion has fallen as a result of the new psychology has served to discredit the old emotional revivalism. The type of evangelistic minister, who believed that there was a place in every sermon where the preacher should drill for water, no longer is found in the principal pulpits of the historic evangelical Churches. As one of my colleagues has recently stated it,

So many sermons sound as if the minister were fearful of revealing any profound emotional tides in his life or faith.[1]

In fact emotion has been so completely squeezed out of present-day Protestant worship that the people are becoming emotionally starved. Perhaps this is one of the reasons why moving pictures are so popular; there, one can be as emotional as one pleases, for it is dark and tears are not noticed.

---

[1] Daniel D. Williams, "Kindled Affections" (*Chicago Theological Seminary Register*, January 1943), 3–6.

How alive today are some of the statements of Jonathan Edwards in his *Treatise on Religious Affections!* In his day none was more aware of the dangers of overemotionalized religion than was he and yet he could not escape the conclusion that the very essence of religion "consists in holy affection." "True religion," he stated, "is a powerful thing . . . a ferment, a vigorous engagedness of the heart." And so it is.

Nearly a generation ago there was a brilliant book published on the Renaissance and the Reformation. The author treated the Renaissance as a series of revivals; there was the revival of learning; the revival of literature; the revival of Art; but the basis revival; the one primarily responsible for all the other revivals, was the *Revival of the Individual.* The author stated that "Society . . . derives its life from individuals who compose it. . . . The individual man remains forever separate . . . he is incapable of fusion. Individuality, the force of separate selfhood, is the most important fact in human life. . . ."[2]

Revivalism, as it has run its course in America, has been primarily the individualizing of religion. It has often been blind to the sins of society, sins which cannot be reached by merely converting individuals. But if religion is to continue as a vital force in America, it must not lose the personal and individual emphasis. At the same time it must concern itself about the sins of society.

---

[2] Edward M. Hulme, *The Renaissance, the Protestant Reformation and the Catholic Reformation in Continental Europe.* Revised Edition (New York, 1915), especially chapter iv, "The Revival of the Individual." "Individuality [was] the most important factor of the Renaissance," 71.

SELECTED BIBLIOGRAPHY

Alexander, Archibald, *Biographical Sketches of the Founder and Principal Alumni of the Log College: Together with an Account of the Revivals of Religion under their Ministry* (Philadelphia, 1851).

Armstrong, Maurice W., *The Great Awakening in Nova Scotia 1759–1809.* (Typed Ph.D. Thesis, Harvard University, 1944).

Asbury, Francis, *Journal of,* 3 vols. (New York, 1853).

Bangs, Nathan, *The Life of the Rev. Freeborn Garrettson: compiled and from his Printed and Manuscript Journals, etc.* (New York, 1829).

Barnes, Gilbert H., *The Anti-Slavery Impulse, 1830–1844* (New York, 1933).

Barnes, Gilbert H., and Dumond, Dwight L., Editors, *Letters of Theodore Dwight Weld, Angelina Grimke Weld and Sarah Grimke, 1822–1844,* 2 vols. (New York, 1934).

Beecher, Lyman, *Autobiography, Correspondence, etc.* Edited by Charles Beecher, 2 vols. (New York, 1866).

Belden, A. D., *George Whitefield: The Awakener* (Nashville, 1930).

Bost, George H., *Samuel Davies, Colonial Revivalist and Champion of Religious Toleration* (Typed Ph.D. Thesis, University of Chicago, 1942).

Bradford, Gamaliel, *D. L. Moody, A Worker in Souls* (New York, 1927).

Branch, E. Douglas, *The Sentimental Years, 1830–1860* (New York, 1934).

Bushnell, Horace, *Christian Nurture* (First Edition, 1847; New York, 1904).

———, *Barbarism, the First Danger: A Discourse for Home Missions* (Pamphlet), (New York, 1847).

Cartwright, Peter, *Autobiography* (New York, 1856).

Chauncy, Charles, *Seasonable Thoughts on the State of Religion in New England* (Boston, 1743).

————, *The Late Religious Commotions in New England Considered: An answer to the Reverend Jonathan Edwards' Sermon entitled,* "The Distinguishing marks of a Work of the Spirit of God. . . ." (Boston, 1743).

Clark, Elmer T., *The Small Sects in America* (Nashville, 1937).

Cleveland, Catherine C., *The Great Revival in the West, 1797–1805* (Chicago, 1916).

Cunningham, Charles E., *Timothy Dwight, 1752–1817. A Biography* (New York, 1942).

Curnock, Nehemiah, Ed., *The Journal of the Reverend John Wesley*, etc., 8 vols. (London, 1909–1916).

Davenport, F. M., *Primitive Traits in Religious Revivals* (New York, 1905).

Davenport, W. W., *The Scripturalness and Expediency of the System of Modern Evangelism* (Boston, 1869).

Davies, Samuel, *Sermons on Important Subjects,* 4 vols. (London, 1815).

Davidson, Robert, *History of Presbyterianism in the State of Kentucky* (New York, 1847).

Dickinson, Jonathan, *The True Scriptural Doctrine concerning some Important Points of Christian Faith* (Boston, 1742; reprinted in Philadelphia, 1876).

————, *A Display of God's Special Grace, in a familiar Dialogue, between a Minister and a Gentleman of his Congregation about the Work of God in the Conviction and Conversion of Sinners,* etc. . . . (Printed anonymously, Boston, 1742; reprinted under the author's name, Philadelphia, 1743).

Earle, A. B., *Bringing in the Sheaves* (Boston, 1868).

Edwards, Jonathan, *A Treatise Concerning Religious Affections, in Three Parts* (Boston, 1746).

————, *Thoughts on the Revival of Religion in New England, to which is prefixed A Narrative of the Surprising Work of God in Northampton, Mass., 1735* (Boston).

————, *The Works of President Edwards*. Ten Volumes (New York, 1830). Also numerous other editions.

Ellis, W. T., *Billy Sunday: The Man and His Message* (Philadelphia, 1914).

Finley, James B., *Autobiography of, or Pioneer Life in the West* (Edited by W. P. Strickland) (Cincinnati, 1857).

————, *Sketches of Western Methodism, Biographical, Historical and Miscellaneous; Illustrative of Pioneer Life*. (Edited by W. P. Strickland) (New York, 1854).

Finney, Charles G., *Lectures on Revivals of Religion* (2nd Ed.) (New York, 1835).

————, *Sermons on Important Subjects* (New York, 1856).

————, *Memoirs of* (New York, 1876).

————, *Guide to the Saviour or Conditions of attaining to and abiding in entire Holiness of Heart and Life* (2nd Ed.) (Oberlin, 1849).

————, *Sermons on Gospel Themes* (Oberlin, 1876).

Gaddis, Merrill E., *Christian Perfectionism in America* (Typed Ph.D. Thesis, The University of Chicago, 1929).

Gewehr, W. M., *The Great Awakening in Virginia* (Durham, N. C., 1930).

Gledstone, James P., *The Life and Travels of George Whitefield, M.A.* (London, 1871).

————, *George Whitefield M.A., Field Preacher* (New York, 1901).

Gospel News, or A Brief Account of the Revival of Religion in Kentucky and Several other parts of the United States . . . (Baltimore, 1801).

Hall, Thomas C., *The Religious Background of American Culture* (Boston, 1930).

Hervey, G. W., *Manual of Revivals: Practical Hints and Suggestions, etc. . . . Including the Texts, Subjects, and Outlines of the Sermons of many Distinguished Evangelists* (New York, 1884).

186   *REVIVALISM IN AMERICA*

Howard, Malcolm, *Evangelism: The Individual and Universal Duty of Christians* (Philadelphia, 1859).

James, William, *The Varieties of Religious Experience* (1st Ed.), 1902) (New York, 1925).

Jarratt, Devereux, *Life of Devereux Jarratt* (Baltimore, 1806).

————, *Sermons on Various and Important Subjects, in Practical Divinity, adapted to the Plainest Capacities, and to the Family and Closet,* 3 vols. (Philadelphia, 1793; Raleigh, 1805).

Johnson, Herrick, *Revivals: Their Place and their Power* (Chicago, 1882).

Lednum, John, *History of the Rise of Methodism in America, containing Sketches of Methodist Itinerant Preachers from 1736–1785* (Philadelphia, 1859).

Leyburn, James G., *Frontier Folkways* (New Haven, 1935).

Loud, Grover C., *Evangelized America* (New York, 1928).

McNemar, Richard, *The Kentucky Revival: or a Short History of the Late Extraordinary Out-pouring of the Spirit of God in . . . America . . .* etc. (Cincinnati, 1807).

Maffitt, John N., *Tears of Contrition, or Sketches of the Life of John N. Maffitt* (New London, Conn., 1821).

————, *Pulpit Sketches* (Louisville, 1839).

Maxson, C. H., *The Great Awakening in the Middle Colonies* (Chicago, 1920).

Mead, Sidney E., *Nathaniel William Taylor, 1786–1858* (Chicago, 1942).

Mecklin, John M., *The Story of American Dissent* (New York, 1934).

Mode, Peter G., *The Frontier Spirit in American Christianity* (New York, 1923).

Moody, D. L., *Gospel Awakenings* (16th Ed.) (Chicago, 1883).

Moody, W. R., *The Life of Dwight L. Moody* (New York, 1930).

Nevin, J. W., *The Anxious Bench—A Tract for the Times* (1843).

Nevins, Allan, "The Emergence of Modern America" (New York, 1927) (Vol. VIII, *A History of American Life*).

Nettleton, Asahel (Compiler), *Village Hymns for Social Worship —Selected and Original—Designed as a supplement to the Psalms and Hymns of Dr. Watts* (Hartford, 1850).

Northridge, W. L., *Recent Psychology and Evangelistic Preaching* (London, 1924).

Nottingham, Elizabeth K., *Methodism and the Frontier: Indiana Proving Ground* (New York, 1941).

Posey, W. B., *The Development of Methodism in the Old Northwest, 1783–1824* (Tuscaloosa, 1933).

Pratt, James B., *The Religious Consciousness: A Psychological Study* (New York, 1920).

Prince, Thomas, *Christian History, containing Accounts of the Revival and Propaganda of Religion in Great Britain and America* (Published weekly from March 5, 1743, to February 23, 1744/45).

Revival of 1858, The New York Pulpit in the . . . A Memorial Volume of Sermons (New York, 1860).

Rice, David, *A Sermon on the Present Revival of Religion, etc. . . . in this Country.* Preached at the opening of the Kentucky Synod, 1803 (Lexington, 1804).

Schlesinger, Arthur M., and Fox, Dixon Ryan (Editors, *A History of American Life*, 12 vols. (New York, 1927).

————, *The Rise of the City, 1878–1898* (New York, 1933) (Vol. IX, *History of American Life*).

Scott, Orange, *The New and Improved Camp-Meeting Hymn Book, etc.* (Brookfield, 1832).

Seldes, Gilbert, *The Stammering Century* (New York, 1928).

Speer, William, *The Great Revival of 1800* (Philadelphia, 1872).

Sprague, William B., *Lectures on Revivals of Religion* (2nd Ed) (New York, 1833).

Sweet, W. W., *Men of Zeal: The Romance of American Methodist Beginnings* (New York, 1935).

————, *Religion on the American Frontier.* Vol. I., *The Baptists* (New York, 1931); Vol. II; *The Presbyterians* (New York, 1936); Vol. III, *The Congregationalists* (Chicago, 1939).

Sweet, W. W., *The Makers of Christianity, from John Cotton to Lyman Abbott* (New York, 1933).

Taylor, James B., *Lives of Virginia Baptist Ministers* (Richmond, 1838).

Taylor, John, *The History of Ten Churches* (Frankfort, 1823).

Telford, John, Ed., *The Letters of the Reverend John Wesley*, etc., 8 vols. (London, 1931).

Tennent, Gilbert, *Twenty-Three Sermons upon the Chief End of Man . . . preached in Philadelphia Anno Dom. 1743* (Philadelphia, 1744).

Tipple, E. S., *Francis Asbury, the Prophet of the Long Road* (New York, 1916).

Tracy, Joseph, *A History of the Revival of Religion in the Time of Edwards and Whitefield* (Boston, 1842).

Tyerman, Luke, *The Life of the Rev. George Whitefield*, 2 vols. (New York, 1877).

Tyler, Bennett, *Memoirs of the Life and Character of Rev. Asahel Nettleton* (Boston, 1856).

Weber, H. C., *Evangelism: A Graphic Survey* (New York, 1929).

Webster, Richard, *A History of the Presbyterian Church in America, from its Origin until the Year 1760* etc. (Philadelphia, 1857).

Wieman, H. N., and Regina Westcott Wieman, *Normative Psychology of Religion* (New York, 1935).

Winslow, Ola Elizabeth, *Jonathan Edwards, 1703–1758* (New York, 1940).

Wright, George F., *Charles Grandison Finney* (Boston, 1893).

INDEX

Abbott, Benjamin, 96, 102–103

Abraham, migration of, 6–7

Adams, Charles Francis, quoted, 9–10

Adams, John, 99

Adopting Act (1729), 73, 74

Alexander, Archibald, 119, defines a true revival, 125–126

Anglican church, clergy oppose Jarratt, 89; effect of the lack of colonial bishops on, 15; in Virginia, 87, 88; under control of planter aristocracy, 23

Anti-slavery movement, and revivalism, 152–159; Wilberforce and, 153; John Wesley and, 153

Arminianism, 128

Asbury, Francis, 96, 100; and the camp meeting, 129–131

Baal, worship of, 7, 10

Baptists, 25, 117, 125, 163; associations, 128; congregational meetings, 133; discipline, 133; farmer-preachers, 91–95; and frontier revivalism, 128; leadership in religious liberty, 42–43; phase of southern colonial revivals, 37–39; position on slavery, 155, 156; Southern and present day revivalism, 175

Beecher, Lyman, 126–127; opposes Finney methods, 135, 137; plea for education, 150–151, 158

Benevolent agencies, and revivalism, 159–160

Bethesda Orphanage, 33

Blair, Samuel, Log College evangelist, 36, 62–64

Bowne, Borden P., quoted, 145

Brenner, Anita, quoted, 11

Brown University (The College of Rhode Island), 147

Buckingham, Stephen, 21

Bundling, 10

Burr, Aaron, 44, 148

Bushnell, Horace, quoted, 2–3, 9, 116

Calvin, John, 23, 40

Calvinism, personalizing of, 28, 29, 30, 124, 127, 128, 135; a legalistic system, 20; and revivalism, 128; and revivals in New England, 30–32; Whitefield's, 106, 107

Calvinists, outstanding revivalists, 28

Camp meetings, become an unofficial Methodist institution, 129–130; begun by Presbyterians, 122; Cane Ridge, 122–123, 124; confusion and disorder of, 142–143; songs, 143–144; transformation of, 165–167

Castellux, Marquis de, *Travels in North America*, 4–5

Chauncy, Charles, arguments against revivalism, 142–143

Chautauqua, development of, 166–167

Chesterton, G. K., 23

Church government, and democracy in the colonies, 42–43

Church membership, among the colonists, 13–19; effect on colonial awakenings, 19; since 1900, xiii

Church and State, separation of, 38

City, the rise of and revivalism, 162, 167–168

Class meetings, 133, 134; class tickets, 134

Classis of Amsterdam, 52

Clergy, cultural changes among, 163, 164

College of New Jersey (Princeton), 34, 147; first five presidents revivalists, 148

College revivalism, 171–172

Colleges, founding related to revivalism, 147, 151; Presbyterian influence in founding, 149; Congregational, 149; Baptist, 149; Methodist, 149

Colonies, cultural level of, 4–6; decline of religion in, 24; lay influence in, 19–20; leadership in, 4; manners and morals in, 2–10; personalization of religion in, 19–21; Pietism in the colonial awakenings, 24–25; preaching in, 20–21

Colonists, economic level of, 5–6; effects of pioneering on, 6

Columbia (King's College), 147

Communion practices among Presbyterians, 132–133